W9-DBD-756

THE HIDDEN WEALTH OF
CUSTOMERS

THE HIDDEN WEALTH OF
CUSTOMERS

Realizing the Untapped Value

of Your Most Important Asset

BILL LEE

HARVARD BUSINESS REVIEW PRESS

BOSTON, MASSACHUSETTS

Printed in the United States of America
10 9 8 7 6 5 4 3 2 1

Library of Congress Cataloging-in-Publication Data

Lee, William G.
    The hidden wealth of customers : realizing the untapped value of your most impor-
tant asset / Bill Lee.
        p. cm.
    ISBN 978-1-4221-7231-5 (alk. paper)
    1. Customer relations.   2. Customer loyalty.   3. Consumer behavior.   I. Title.
    HF5415.5.L43 2012
    658.8'342—dc23

                                                                    2011053278

The paper used in this publication meets the requirements of the American National
Standard for Permanence of Paper for Publications and Documents in Libraries and
Archives Z39.48-1992

CONTENTS

1

The Coming Customer Revolution

Transforming Customers into Advocates, Influencers, and Contributors

I N THE LAST DECADE, many companies have undergone a tidal shift in focus toward the customer as key to their firm's vigor and sustainable growth. Certainly business writing has reflected and supported this proposition—yet the focus remains shortsighted.[1] Companies sink lots of resources into improving customer relationships and creating customer promoters with a very limited goal: to induce them to buy more stuff. Yet the act of buying is just one way—and often not the most lucrative way—that customers can create value. In fact, by focusing so single-mindedly on such a narrow goal, companies shortchange both their customers and themselves.

The fact is that businesses today need a more reliable way to grow. Particularly in a foundering world economy, what's needed is robust organic growth—that is, growth generated by the firm's own product development, marketing, sales, services, and other internal resources.

This book goes beyond the limited purview of customer-as-buyer to show you how to unlock the value of customer relationships in all of the firm's internal growth processes. It's a book about reimagining the source of true wealth creation: the customer value proposition. Drawing from a wide range of case studies and company examples, this book will show you how to engage with, organize, and leverage the force of your own customer base to propel sustained growth—all while creating far greater value for customers themselves.

Hidden in Plain Sight: Today's Greatest Overlooked Growth Opportunity

The traditional business growth engine consists of some combination of research, product development, marketing, sales, and service—all run by employees. The best way to get more growth, it's assumed, is to hire employees who excel in the disciplines of research, product development and design, sales, marketing, and service.

That traditional, often unquestioned, approach overlooks your most valuable growth asset by far—particularly in today's hyperconnected world: your own customers. Why? Figure 1-1 illustrates how most firms see themselves vis-à-vis their customers and their market, whereas figure 1-2 shows the hidden reality.

FIGURE 1-1

How most companies see themselves and their customers and market

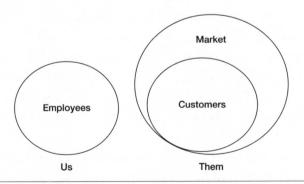

FIGURE 1-2

Here's the reality—and the opportunity

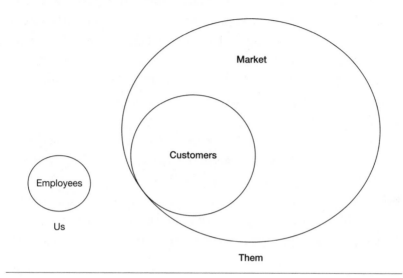

To put it into words, when it comes to their customers, the companies you'll read about in this book have realized the following:

- There are a lot more of them than us.

- Their day-to-day world is a lot different from ours, and we'll never fully understand it like they do.

- They have far more credibility with other customers and prospects than we do.

- Some of them understand buyer needs far better than we ever will.

- They would rather associate with each other (their peers) than with us.

- The Internet and social media are making this increasingly easy to do.

Therefore, the new thinking goes, companies need to overcome the "us and them" approach and bring "them" into their growth-generating processes. That is, into their marketing processes (customers have more credibility than we do), into their sales processes (better understanding of buyer needs), and into their product development processes (better understanding of buyers' day-to-day world). For more and more of these businesses, "them" refers to those exceptional customers—the "rock stars"—who can rapidly accelerate growth (figure 1-3). The time to get serious about this is *now,* when social media and the Web are making this change increasingly possible.

You can learn to cultivate the most value from your hard-won customer relationships. You can learn to maximize *and measure* what I call the return on relationship (ROR) with customers. You can learn to identify and integrate your rock star customers in ways that foster a robust virtuous cycle in which you provide them with far more value, and they, in turn, enrich your company. How? Through

FIGURE 1-3

Bring "rock star" customers into growth processes

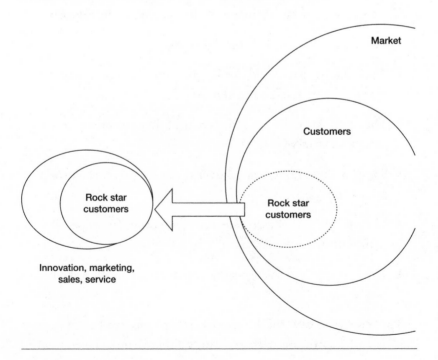

nothing less than a revolution in the way you and your customers do business—a revolution that's already well under way at many companies profiled in this book.

Let's begin with a closer look at that revolutionary new value proposition, after which I'll illustrate how the software company Salesforce.com enjoys rapid organic growth while offering more value to customers. Then we will explore how the new value proposition in turn fosters critical customer relationships, the best of which, with your rock stars, are your key to organic growth. I'll provide a number of examples from companies I've seen and worked with that illustrate how this new proposition is starting to take hold.

Later in the chapter, I touch briefly on how these elements work together to improve a firm's ROR with customers. Finally, I outline a road map for *The Hidden Wealth of Customers* and how each chapter of the book will unfold.

A New Customer Value Proposition

After a customer completes a purchase, what is typically left on the table is a gold mine of ways that firms can increase both the value they provide for customers and the profitability customers generate for the firm. With the new customer value proposition, you essentially reinvent your relationship, transforming customers into what I call customer advocates, influencers, and contributors (AICs). The following story illustrates what I'm talking about.

Unleashing a Hidden Rock Star

Let's say you have a customer named Catie, who has shown some clear signs of being an outstanding, and probably underused, customer advocate. In Net Promoter Score (NPS) surveys, she regularly says she's a "promoter" of your firm, she's a member of several associations that you're interested in, and she's an avid social media networker.

As you begin to engage with Catie, you find that she's quite open to an advocacy role. Therefore—this is critical—you work with her to create a strong, mutual exchange of value based on her personal and professional goals. This is not about crass rewards or bribes to encourage an ambivalent customer to say great things about you. It's about working with a customer who's passionate about the products and services you provide in order to tell the story of the great things she's doing, with your help, to improve her business.

Catie's value is further enhanced when you learn that she is keen to expand her network and reputation within her industry, which cuts across a number of smaller industries in which your firm, too, happens to be interested.

Putting that information together launches Catie to rock stardom over the next year, as you begin to feed Catie new product and industry information, plus relevant thought leadership from your internal experts. She responds by blogging and tweeting this information and, when appropriate, mentioning your firm and providing links to further relevant information you provide. She is also able to respond with positive comments, based on her own experience, to any negative asides that might flame through. As a result, easily obtained social media measurements show an increase in the conversation about your firm, including an increase in the positive comments.

From there you can expand this new partnership with Catie to include videos and Webinars that you produce together on how her business is succeeding as a result of smart choices she's made with your help. As you build your network of rock stars, you arrange regular local events and an annual conference to bring such advocates together with prospects and media people, events that turn out to be terrific sales vehicles. What's more, your thought leadership—which focuses on your knowledge of Catie's industry to show how to succeed therein—leads you and Catie in yet further new directions.

Customers like Catie can generate tremendous value beyond anything they purchase. In the next chapter, you'll learn more about specific ways to nurture your relationship with customers like Catie and how to assess their value. My point for now is that all of these activities represent tangible, high-value creation—value that most companies fail either to foster or measure.

If You Think You're Already Doing This

You may say that you already do regular, rigorous customer surveys to gauge customer experience and loyalty. Perhaps you're an ardent user of the NPS system, and your customers tell you repeatedly that they'd be "highly likely" to recommend you to others. You work hard at creating more such promoters, based on the critical metric, made famous by Bain Consulting's Fred Reichheld, that identifies your most loyal customers as those most likely to recommend you to others.[2] (See the sidebar "After NPS: The Next Step.") You might tick off your company's various initiatives, such as a customer reference program, customer advisory boards, and user groups, and point to these as confirmation that your company brings customers into its product or solution development process as well.

But do your business results, your growth, reflect all of that work? Do you have, for example, a way to ensure that referrals happen? How do you measure the results? In my own observation and work that I do with firms—including those with a laundry list of formal customer programs—I've found that many have major gaps and missed opportunities that add up to serious losses of potential earnings. They may work diligently and effectively to create promoters, yet do nothing to encourage them to, well, *promote*—whether through referrals, testimonials, speaking at industry events, participation in a white paper or case study, or so forth. And they do even less to actually bring customers into their product development processes.

At least one respected firm that uses NPS *and* had a customer reference program, SAP, found that the customer references in its database were *not* the same customers as those who self-identified as promoters.

Why Customer Engagement Programs Fail

Even for firms that do provide customers with opportunities to promote them—such as with a formal customer reference program, for example—can miss many opportunities. Many customer

After NPS: The Next Step

No business thinker has done more than Bain Consulting's Fred Reichheld to demonstrate the importance of loyal customers—and, in particular, customer advocacy—to sustained organic business growth. His most recent contribution, Net Promoter Score (NPS), emphasizes the link between these two concepts: your most loyal customers are the ones who are most likely to recommend you to a colleague or friend, and thus are called *promoters.*

Initial research across a number of industries has shown that companies who have the highest NPS tend to have the highest profitability and market share in their industries.[a] However, subsequent research hasn't always confirmed such stellar results, and the reason why seems clear. Firms that concentrate solely on customer loyalty or their NPS typically don't do anything special to *bring their promoters into their marketing and sales efforts.* By not doing so, they're leaving economic value on the table. Promoters who, after all, are merely *saying* in a survey that they would be likely to promote your business are, in fact, *not* likely to actually do so.

For example, in research in a telecommunications firm and a financial services firm, only about 10 percent or so of their promoters actually referred prospects who became profitable customers. Put another way, about 90 percent of their promoters weren't actually referring customers that the firms wanted.[b] (See "The truth behind promoters.") Imagine what those 90 percent could do with a bit of help and encouragement. That's pretty much what the rest of this book is about.

engagement programs are underfunded and staffed by junior-level employees with little understanding of corporate strategy—and thus of which customer references to cultivate. Often the staff are overworked and struggle with data systems so inadequate that they can do little more than provide concierge service to sales and mar-

The truth behind promoters

	Telecom	Financial services
"I'll recommend you"	81%	68%
Actually did so	30%	33%
Generated new customers	12%	14%
Profitable new customers	8%	11%

This is the next great opportunity for firms who have built NPS programs or otherwise oriented their business to create passionate customers. Working to create "promoters" doesn't come close to capturing what the companies profiled in this book are doing. It's only the price of admission. Such companies are bringing customers into their sales, marketing, and product development processes to get better product development success rates and higher returns, a lower cost of qualified lead generation, improved sales close rates, and above all, to create rapid awareness, interest, and the desire to buy in marketplaces saturated with information.

This is no magic bullet. It takes hard work and, in particular, significant attention and involvement by senior management while you reinvent the customer relationship. But the rewards, as we'll see, are worth it.

[a] Frederick F. Reichheld, *The Ultimate Question: Driving Good Profits and True Growth* (Boston: Harvard Business School Press, 2006), 188–189.
[b] V. Kumar, J. Andrew Peterson, and Robert P. Leone, "How Valuable Is Word of Mouth?" *Harvard Business Review*, October 2007, 139.

keting people when they're in urgent need of a reference to close a deal or be interviewed by the media. The references such programs acquire are often not the ones that sales and marketing need, and those few references who are needed often suffer from reference burnout.

Other indicators of gaps and missed opportunities in your customer relationships include the following:

- Persistently low new product development success rates

- Lack of creative new ideas generated by advisory boards, or, for those boards that do come up with good ideas, lack of follow-through in implementing them

- Inability of firms to build their own successful customer communities, settling instead for engaging customers through other social media groups; and failure to track or even encourage customer referrals

- Failure to integrate various customer engagement efforts based on a compelling, holistic value proposition to customers, leading to customer confusion, dissatisfaction, and burnout

All of this is to say that, in a world economic environment where markets have shifted seismically, companies today don't seem to recognize an all-too-obvious truth: they continue to do business based on an antiquated customer value proposition that offers too few returns.

The time has come to move beyond delighting customers or measuring their loyalty. Companies need to ask themselves, Are we doing all we can to tap the hidden value that we can harvest from our customers and that they can gain from us? The appendix of this book contains a complete diagnostic that will help you answer that question for your company and measure how far it falls short.

Reinventing Your Customer Relationships

How do companies begin the process of engaging customers in a deep and meaningful way? Salesforce.com, National Instruments, SAS Institute, Wells Fargo, Coca-Cola, and other companies have already begun expanding the value they provide customers, through offerings such as opportunities to gain recognition and status in their industry, engage with vibrant peer communities, and participate in industry thought leadership. They are in turn grooming such customers to create exceptional reciprocal value beyond the price paid for a product or service. (See figures 1-4 and 1-5.)

FIGURE 1-4

Typical customer initiatives, which have one objective: to get customers to purchase

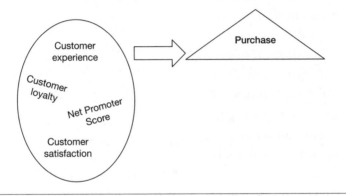

FIGURE 1-5

Realizing your company's full return on relationship: there are many more ways in which customers can create value

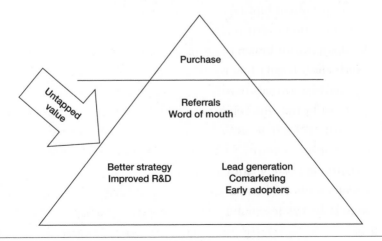

Companies that follow suit on this new customer value proposition will find that, when properly engaged and managed, customers will actively recommend the company, and firms will be able to measure those results.

But that's only the beginning. Engaged customers will take other steps too, such as

- Saying positive things about you to the media, building awareness and brand

- Speaking at industry conferences about the things they're doing with your products and services

- Appearing in your advertising and branding efforts—and providing far more credible testimonials than anything your copywriters or company spokespeople could say

- Referring other buyers to you, taking calls, and accepting site visits from your sales prospects to help close deals

- Participating in your customer advisory boards to keep your R&D efforts grounded in the reality of *customers'* changing needs—rather than the product features your engineers desire

- Having key-customer executives participate in higher-level forums and communities to help keep your strategy focused on top customer issues

What's more, in the exploding new world of social media, your customers will engage with your market, say more nice things about you, and counter the negative comments you can no longer control or edit out. And they'll do these things with far more credibility than any spokesperson or salesperson could muster, demonstrating the truth of the adage that "The best person to find your next customer is a current customer."

All of this points to an emerging new phase of business marketing, what is increasingly being called *community marketing,* in which people *outside* the firm—not just your product developers and marketers—become deeply engaged in a shared conversation that addresses the needs of customers.

Let's look now at a case study of how Salesforce.com is already tapping the hidden wealth that its customers have to share, for mutual benefit.

How Customer Advocates Built a Billion-Dollar Business: The Case of Salesforce.com

About a decade ago, a brash entrepreneur named Marc Benioff decided to start a firm that would challenge the entire software industry.[3] He knew he couldn't match the marketing or development budgets of his competitors—multibillion-dollar firms such as Oracle, SAP, and Seibel. There was no way. Instead, he would have to rely from the first on his customers to help. His new firm, Salesforce.com (SFDC), would rely on customers for almost everything: to help develop its software and to help brand, market, sell, and continue to improve it. In return, his firm would have to provide them an extraordinary value proposition.

The result was arguably the most successful business technology firm in the world over the last decade. The stories of Benioff's good-natured, in-your-face PR efforts, such as "declaring war" on traditional enterprise software, picketing competitors' events with "No Software" signs, and the like, are well known. More remarkable, and more relevant to business today, is how he achieved rapid growth so quickly by tapping the vast wealth customers could create, beyond just buying the company's products and services.

Recruiting Customers as Design Partners

From the first, Benioff and his team worked closely with prospective customers to develop the firm's new customer relationship management (CRM) service. He already had a good idea, from previous experience in the industry, about why traditional enterprise systems were not serving customers well: they required massive up-front investment, most of these investments wound up not paying off, and upgrades were often so difficult that customers would forego the improvements to avoid the hassle of trying to make them work.

But it was in interactions with potential customers that Benioff and his team made sure they could provide a compelling alternative. One prospect, a family friend, tried the system and provided constant reminders to make it easier to navigate, with as few clicks as possible. Other friends from Cisco, who were also prospects, shared with Benioff the details of what they despised about traditional enterprise software—prompting Benioff to offer a monthly licensing model, no long-term contract, and no big up-front fee. He also hired a firm to get additional feedback and videotape users, thereby uncovering more opportunities to improve the platform.

This iterative process of bringing prospective customers into the development of the firm's CRM service continued when the first version was ready for beta release. Benioff called these customers "design partners," an indication of how differently he viewed the relationship—he was designing a product *with* customers rather than testing it *on* them. He and his engineers talked to customers frequently to continue refining and improving their experience. For example, they created a button that users could click to send ideas for improvements directly to SFDC, as well as a database called "bugforce" to track bugs that arose as well as new ideas submitted by users. This constant interaction allowed the SFDC development team to complete the additional functionality in weeks, rather than the months or longer typical in the industry.

Generating Rapid Growth: Holding Live Events with "Rock Stars"

When SFDC was released to the public, Benioff and his team quickly looked for ways to engage with its new customers to help get the word out and promote its service—laying the groundwork for a highly efficient growth engine. They started with a six-stop "City Tour" that brought customers together with prospects, analysts, and the media. The first event, in Philadelphia, attracted just fifteen of the fifty people who were invited, but Benioff and his executives saw the remarkable energy that these early events generated—not because customers and prospects were meeting SFDC executives, but because they got the chance to meet and talk to *each other.* As SFDC got better at harnessing that energy, the City Tour events grew quickly and became essential to the exceptional word of mouth that SFDC generated. Eighty percent of prospects who attended City Tour events became customers.

By continuing to engage customers and build advocacy, Benioff achieved rapid growth for the upstart business. The firm's attention-getting PR efforts, augmented by live encounters with customers and strong word of mouth, drove prospects to its Web site, where Benioff saw the potential to offer customers more than the usual brochureware that was "all about us." He designed the Salesforce.com site instead to highlight the company's "rock star" customers, identifying SFDC's most dynamic advocates and using their stories and testimonials to educate prospects and guide them through the buying process in compelling ways.

Such customer advocacy and engagement efforts weren't just to get the firm going—creating rock stars has been central to the firm's strategy for growth throughout its journey to $1 billion in sales and continues as its guiding organizational principle. After all, as the firm has grown, customers have become more plentiful—and far more credible—than in-house sales and marketing people.

To the City Tour events, SFDC added an array of other events, including more intimate local events that created just as many high-value leads with prospective customers and closed deals, but at a fraction of the cost. To his surprise, Benioff discovered that simply bringing customers together, even without any sort of formal presentation, was as effective for closing deals as the City Tour stops had been—confirming that buyers and customers valued interactions with each other above all. The company also inaugurated its annual user conference, called Dreamforce, which drew one thousand people in the firm's third year and has spawned thousands of customer advocates over the years. By observing customers in action at these events, SFDC continues to identify which are most passionate about its service and most effective at telling others about it. The company then engages with these rock stars to provide testimonials, case studies, and videos and to serve as speakers at industry events.

To manage all of these efforts, the firm built a formal customer reference program (CRP). Unlike other firms that often regard company events as just one in a long checklist of sales and marketing initiatives, SFDC placed references at the *center* of sales and marketing. For example, three of the five things that SFDC's salespeople are trained to say in "a winning sales call" depend on the CRP (the three are as follows: provide success stories from customers; verify those success stories with customer testimonials; and provide a customer for the prospect to contact).

Leveraging Live Events with Social Media

SFDC continues to hone its ability to engage customers and prospects in increasingly creative ways, arguably its greatest competitive advantage. In 2008, it developed a Facebook-like platform called Chatter that allows attendees at Dreamforce to engage with each other before the conference, form their own groups, make plans to meet at the conference, and exchange knowledge, including PowerPoint decks (the business equivalent of exchanging pictures on Facebook).

The firm attributes to Chatter the substantially increased growth rate of Dreamforce attendance, despite the recession. Perhaps the most vivid sign of the consistent, rapid growth of a firm built on customer advocacy is the 40,000-plus attendees who registered for Dreamforce in 2011.

To understand how companies such as SFDC enjoy rapid organic growth while offering more value to customers, we'll look now in more detail at the old customer value proposition versus the new one.

The Old Versus New Customer Value Propositions

Traditionally, business has seen its role as producing products or services that help a customer get a job done. In return, the customer pays money (figure 1-6).

In today's world, that value proposition is becoming terribly old-fashioned. As I've pointed out, typical customer initiatives today do nothing to expand the notion of value a company can provide its customers. They focus instead on "delighting" the customer, or providing a memorable experience to the customer—but only to support the narrow process of helping him or her get a particular job done.

Firms such as Microsoft, Coca-Cola, and SFDC are helping customers gain greater insight and understanding, and expand their personal networks, in their own industries. Such an enhanced value offering will be key to building customer advocacy in the next decade and is already an area of tremendous creativity.

SFDC, for instance, created substantial new value for the end users of its platform—a group traditionally ignored by established enterprise software firms, which focused instead on the higher-level decision makers. For example, the company publicly recognized and celebrated the end users—or "heroes"—who used the SFDC platform in creative ways, focusing especially on those who did so

FIGURE 1-6

The old customer value proposition

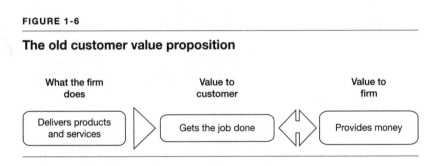

What the firm does	Value to customer	Value to firm
Delivers products and services	Gets the job done	Provides money

to create positive business results for their firms. The company also created an SFDC certification that helped end users gain greater recognition within their firms. Over time, these end users began touting their certification and recognition on their resumes, and Benioff noticed that Monster.com began to advertise jobs for programmers who were certified on the SFDC platform. The result of the company's creative approaches was to create both demand for end users on the job market as well as greater interest and awareness of SFDC among management.

Now think of the value—professional, personal, emotional—that firms such as SFDC and others we'll learn about are creating for customers, as opposed to what customers had been getting from traditional software firms (figure 1-7).

This expanded customer value proposition is worth pondering. It helps you to look beyond the rational benefits that companies can provide to customers to the *emotional* benefits companies can

FIGURE 1-7

The new customer value proposition

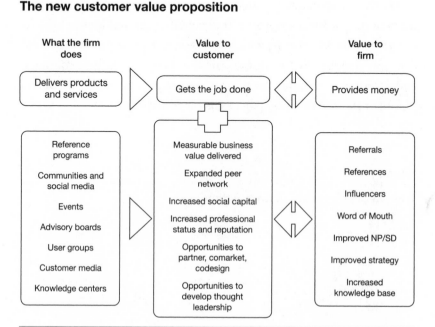

offer. Whereas rational benefits get customers to *think about* engaging in new ways with firms, emotional benefits get customers to *act.* For example, customers of the firms we profile here report that these expanded customer offerings help them in the following ways:

- "Make my life easier"

- "Improve my job security"

- "Advance my career"

- "Find community"

- "Engage with my peers—people who really understand me"

- "Gain status and respect"

- "Learn and grow"

We might call this the "Care and Feeding List for Customer Rock Stars." Compare that list to the important but comparatively tepid benefits customers gain from simply getting a job done, and you begin to understand how the new customer value proposition creates the kinds of customer AICs (advocates, influencers, and contributors) that are key to business wealth creation today.

Toward Improving Return on Relationship

In their efforts to bring products and services to market, companies typically employ product developers—engineers, designers, and researchers—to innovate and improve the firm's offerings. They employ marketers to position and explain the offerings to customers and prospects and entice them to buy, and they employ salespeople to engage personally with customers and close deals. All three of these groups have one thing in common: they can never really understand customers because they're not customers themselves. Organizations that achieve rapid growth don't get there with that business model.

If you look at companies that are achieving profitable growth, such as Salesforce.com, Apple, Facebook, Hitachi Data Systems, and others, you'll find that customer advocacy and evangelism play an essential role. They have to. It is simply too easy for buyers to find out about you before you ever reach them with a marketing message or sales call, and their preferred way of doing so is by talking to their peers who are already doing business with you—that is, your customers.

In the future, great product developers, marketers, and sales-people will be judged not by how well they innovate, market, and sell per se, but instead by how successfully they *bring customers into these processes* in ways that spur robust growth.

It bears repeating that the return on relationship that companies stand to gain from customers is part of a larger equation, a virtuous cycle in which firms improve what they offer customers, which allows customers to gain more value from firms' products and services and thereby improves what customers can offer companies. The following subsections set forth a more comprehensive list of the kinds of business results that are emerging from robust customer engagement efforts at SFDC and other companies profiled in this book.

Customer Salespeople

As we've seen, SFDC builds tours of local events around its customer advocates, in which the advocates mix with prospects and other influencers, exchange ideas, and ultimately do the firm's selling for it, resulting in up to 80 percent close rates at these events for an approximate cost of $250 per person.

Improved Sales Productivity

Even with a conventional sales approach, a well-organized customer reference program will provide salespeople with the right reference at the right time to help move deals. We'll see how a midsized enterprise software firm found that its customer reference program returns five dollars in increased revenue for every dollar invested.

Creative Uses of Social Media

You'll see how SFDC uses its Facebook-like platform, Chatter, to capture essential features of today's most popular social media platform so as to facilitate community building by its customers while building interest in its annual customer event, Dreamforce. SFDC credits Chatter for exponential growth of Dreamforce during the recent extended recession. Prior to implementing Chatter, Dreamforce was growing at a rate of 30 percent per year. Since then (in 2009, 2010, and 2011) it's been growing at a rate of 60 percent per year, despite the stagnant economy.

Improved—and Inexpensive—Lead Generation

Intel credits well-designed testimonials and other customer content for an explosion in the creation of qualified prospective customer interest and inquiries. The company can't share the numbers publicly, but we can say that within a few years, it expects to bring in a significant percentage of all its new business through its Web site efforts—and the key to this growth is content from its existing customers. In 2011, SFDC cut traditional lead generation spending by 69 percent while increasing spending on customer videos (by 1,300 percent) and social media. The result was an increase in contacts generated by social media of 400 percent.

Successful Customer Community Building

We'll see a number of examples of firms building successful customer communities that contribute increasing value. The CSC WikonnecT community, for example, is increasing customer satisfaction scores, improving new product development efforts, and strengthening the brand, along with increasing acceptance rates for its new software updates to 50 percent—all due to improved communication resulting from this well-engaged community. National Instruments' LabVIEW community resulted in an adoption rate of 60 percent for its new robotics software against an established competitor, almost two and a half times the firm's ambitious goal. Citrix Systems developed one of the highest-selling apps on the Apple App Store by engaging its customer community of lawyers, doctors, and other small business professionals who use its software.

Building Marketing Gravity and Eventually Thought Leadership in Your Market

We'll see how Hitachi Data Systems (HDS) is establishing its own platform for influence and even thought leadership in order to get the word out about its products and services in a competitive and very noisy market. HDS is doing so by engaging its internal experts, including chief technology officer Hu Yoshida, with customers and prospects in creative ways.

Rapid Business Growth Using an Often-Overlooked Customer Source

The referral value of many customers is *greater* than their purchasing value. For instance, a better understanding of which customers generate significant referral value helped to double the effectiveness of marketing campaigns at a telecommunications and a financial services firm.

A Powerful, Inexpensive Way to Penetrate New Markets

Influencer value is a source of wealth for companies that may soon rival that provided by referrals. We'll see, for example, how Microsoft is penetrating foreign markets in which it doesn't speak the language or understand the culture by identifying and engaging with existing influencers in these regions who have already acquired major followings through the Internet and social media.

Improved Engagement with Customer Executives

Engaging with key-customer *executives* can be particularly lucrative for business-to-business (B2B) firms. Studies by the Geehan Group show that firms that specifically target decision makers in customer engagement programs achieve customer retention rates of 90 percent (versus 72 percent for those who don't) and account growth of 12 percent (versus 4 percent). Most remarkably, customer executives who are so engaged are far more likely to participate in referral activities: 94 percent versus 28 percent.[4]

We'll see how industry councils developed by Microsoft—using an approach and budget well within the reach of much smaller firms—are enabling the firm to stay at the forefront of important industry needs, build a reputation for industry leadership as well as thought leadership, and, of course, help its executives build strong relationships with influential executives throughout the industry.

Improved R&D and New Product Development

By skillfully engaging in strategy discussions with key-customer executives on its executive advisory boards, Harris Broadcast was able to generate 50 percent of its revenue from products developed within the previous twenty-four months. This was critical for its survival in a competitive environment. We'll also see how 3M multiplied the return on investment of its already respected innovation efforts by engaging with another type of "extended" customer— lead users in its target markets.

Better Retention Rates

SAS Institute (Canada) credits its vigorous customer engagement efforts—which include a combination of a reference program, user groups, key account management, and communities—with restoring its lagging customer retention rates (from 88 percent to a near-perfect 98 percent).

Development of Disruptive Technologies and Growth of Customer Base

Companies such as Salesforce.com, Citrix Systems, and National Instruments are using customer communities and social media to foster innovation and grow their customer bases in remarkable ways. Citrix communities are developing disruptive innovations that show the potential for supplanting entrenched competition and even launching entirely new market opportunities. For example, Citrix challenged the established leader in the server virtualization market, where Citrix had no previous presence or mind share. Using social media together with a new usage-based product strategy, the firm's community Web site generated 150,000 downloads. Downloaders included some 10 percent of the *Fortune* 500, who are now using a version of Citrix's virtualization software. This is a remarkably rapid and inexpensive form of new market penetration.

Customer Contributions of Knowledge

We'll see a variety of ways in which engaged customers gladly contribute remarkable value to the firms with which they do business. Westlaw, for example, has developed a lucrative service called Peer Monitor, based on aggregating information collected from its regular law firm customers that subscribe to its legal information service, that develops exceptionally valuable information about the law firm business—information such as staffing levels and market analysis for use in deciding whether to enter new markets.

Skype has built a well-regarded global communication system using the Internet along with customer laptops to power it. SFDC, Dell, and other technology firms are using community input to prioritize and develop new features—which has proven an effective way to handle the complexities of new feature development for highly heterogeneous customer markets.

A Road Map to This Book

Executives and managers who are focused on their company's growth, particularly CEOs and business unit heads of B2B firms, will find this book an invaluable tool for expanding their value proposition to customers in creative ways, even in companies that already have a number of customer programs. The book will also help executives responsible for delivering on product development, marketing, and sales goals—as well as managers and staff who implement the customer programs that will promote growth.

In chapter 2, we dive straight into the nuts and bolts of ROR: how to foster substantive returns on relationships with customers, including identifying and developing your rock stars—and how to measure that return.

The remainder of the book will show you, using numerous case studies, how to partner with customers to augment (and, in some cases, replace) many company functions and positions that, in the old customer value proposition at least, were key to wealth creation. Chapter 3 illustrates how your customers will sell for you, whereas chapter 4 demonstrates how customers will market for you. Chapter 5 illustrates how customers can help build your Web presence, and in chapter 6 you will see how customers can build whole communities around your product or service. Chapter 7 describes how your C-suite customers can help you with strategy. Finally, chapter 8 helps you identify and nurture key customers who will cocreate or improve products and services with your R&D team—and the chapter concludes with a blueprint for using this book to accelerate your company's growth and win the customers of the future.

Let's begin with how to position your company to ensure that its customer initiatives have a clear and measurable impact on your firm's growth and profitability.

2

Return on Relationship

The Key to Turning Customer Engagement into Organic Growth

SINCE THE TRADITIONAL CUSTOMER value proposition fails to tap the potential of what customers can bring to a company's growth, the value proposition I'm describing in these pages provides a system not only for tapping customers' hidden wealth but also for measuring it. Measurement is critical because just as you want to understand who your most profitable purchasing customers are, you'll also want to understand who your most valuable advocates, influencers, and contributors (AICs) are. As we'll see, you're likely to find that only a few of your customer AICs are contributing the lion's share of value—*and* that they aren't necessarily who you think they are.

That's the subject of this chapter. We'll use a pragmatic, easily installed measurement system—based on the concept of return on relationship (ROR)—that will help focus your company on uncovering and realizing the full value of your customer AICs. But first I'll illustrate how this works.

The Hidden Wealth in Your Midst

Let's return to Catie, our rock star customer from chapter 1. Catie runs a small business, placing her in one of your most important markets, the small and medium business (SMB) market, which presents significant opportunities for growth for your firm.

Catie is not a particularly big revenue customer as far as your business model goes—she spends about $6,000 per year, and generates $2,400 in profit. But she's a potential gold mine nonetheless. To begin with, she's loyal, easy to service, not price sensitive, and, as a result, is solidly profitable—unlike many of your higher-revenue but short-term or difficult-to-work-with customers.

Much more significant, however, is her tremendous hidden wealth. She has a great story to tell about the value your firm provides to her business, typical of what you could be doing for many other businesses in this important market. She consistently selects "9" or "10" on Net Promoter Score (NPS) surveys, indicating that she would be highly likely to recommend your firm to a colleague or friend.

She participates in your online customer community and in other networks attractive to your business. The people who get to know her in these communities appear to respect and engage with her insights and opinions. People pay attention to, comment on, and click the links she provides when she posts or comments on community sites.

She's been to a couple of your live events, and though she tends to say little unless asked, when she does answer, people listen and ask for more. After the events, she hangs around to answer questions from your company's prospects, who are eager to learn from her. Indeed, many of them wind up becoming customers, and if you asked, they'd say Catie was an important reason why. Some would even say that without her influence, they wouldn't have purchased.

Another thing about Catie: she's quite engaged with members of her business network on social media. She keeps a blog, has active

LinkedIn and Facebook pages along with a Twitter account, and frequently blogs, tweets, or comments on developments in her industry as well as profession. A straightforward analysis of her social media presence shows that she's an influencer with attractive ties to excellent prospects for your firm's products and services—many of whom you and your salespeople would love to connect with. Her network on LinkedIn in particular is enough to make your sales and marketing department drool.

Despite all this, your firm, like many firms, doesn't engage with Catie to help market and sell your offerings. The truth is, you're not even aware of her and many others like her. Despite saying quite plainly in NPS surveys that she'd be highly likely to recommend you, that information never makes it from your customer intelligence group to the right sales and marketing people, so Catie is never asked to provide a reference to help further or close a deal. Neither has she provided any referrals to your firm—primarily because no one has asked her to do so.

If you think this couldn't happen at your firm, check out the story about Coleen Kaiser and SAP in chapter 3. Indeed, studies have shown that Catie is typical of customers who score high in NPS surveys: perhaps only 10 percent or so actually refer a colleague or friend who turns out to be a profitable customer.[1] Many more likely would do so if someone would just ask them in the right way.

One other thing about Catie: as you would discover if only your sales and marketing people were building a relationship with her, she's quite ambitious and eager to promote her own stature in her profession, and she wants to extend her growing network of peer and industry relationships. She's interested in overcoming her stage fright and speaking at industry events. She'd be wide open to collaborating on case studies, videos, white papers, interviews with the media, and whatever else could help her grow her network and build her reputation. She would love to tell her peers and customers the great things your firm and she are doing together—because that makes her look good too—if someone would just ask her to do it.

In short, Catie is a potential "rock star" advocate for your firm—the sort of customer who powers the growth of firms such as Salesforce.com, Amazon.com, Hitachi Data Systems, Facebook, and others. She can drive organic growth that "sticks" and bring in new customers who benefit immensely from the value you provide. Your firm could be engaging with her to build a remarkable new exchange of exceptional value, in which you work with her to make her an increasingly powerful evangelist for your firm while helping her build her network, her reputation, and her business. Firms that miss this opportunity—or undermine it by offering poorly disguised bribes to get their customers to advocate for them—are leaving a lot of value, a lot of profits, on the table.

Next we'll look at specific ways that customers like Catie provide value to companies; then I'll show you how to calculate the return on relationship—the impact on firm growth—that such customers can create.

The Hidden Potential of Your Advocates, Influencers, and Contributors

Innovative firms are regularly finding new ways to bring customers into their growth processes—a trend that will likely accelerate as these firms become more adept at finding and engaging with their most fertile customers. To get a handle on this process, let's look at the activities in which customers in our three broad categories—advocates, influencers, and contributors—already engage, or could engage with your encouragement. (Note that these aren't intended as exhaustive lists.)

Advocates

Customer advocates like Catie provide positive information and experiences about your firm to colleagues, their networks, and industry audiences. Here are just some of the things advocates can provide for you:

- Referrals

- References

- Testimonials

- Speaking (that touts what your firm does for them)

- Videos

- Case studies

- Articles

- Interviews

- Blog posts

- Community commentary

- Live events (as evangelists or organizers)

- Teleconferences, Webinars

- Early adoption of your new or less-well-known offerings (which they blog and tweet about)

Influencers

Unlike advocates, influencers are often thought of as experts who take a neutral or objective view. Based on their own test runs or regular use of your products or services, they influence the broader discussion about the jobs or goals that your customers or prospects are trying to achieve, and for which your offerings are intended to help.

Calling or treating an influencer as an advocate can be a bad idea. His objectivity and reputation for objectivity are essential both to him and to the value he can provide to you. This would be the case, for instance, with journalists, analysts, and some bloggers who think of themselves in a similar way. That said, some of your customers who are unabashed fans also wield influence through blogging, article writing, interviews, and so forth. Note that all influencers can be thought of as "customers" in an extended sense, because your goal is to engage in a mutual exchange of value with them.

Influencers disseminate their expert opinions through things such as the following:

- Articles

- Blog posts or comments

- Speaking

- Books

- Interviews

- Webinars

- Attending live events, including industry gatherings and your corporate events

- Hosting events

- Creating an industry publication

- Announcements and commentary on new offerings or strategies

- Testing and commenting on new products or offerings

Contributors

Contributors provide insights or knowledge in a variety of ways, often for free, that helps companies. Contributors can include traditional purchasing customers—such as the book buyers who provide reviews and whose purchases generate data that creates remarkably accurate recommendations useful to other buyers on Amazon.com. They can include law firms that provide firm financial data to Westlaw in exchange for receiving aggregated firm financial data from other firms to help them run their businesses. Customer contributors (and "extended" customers) can also include "lead users," who craft high-value changes to your products or services or outright innovations that they'll often share with your firm, hoping you'll develop them further.

Contributors will offer you tangible help such as the following:

- Feedback or input to improve products or services

- Feedback or input to develop new ones

- Innovations of your products on their own

- Creating apps

- Improving your products and services

- Providing data or information that can add new value to existing offerings or provide the basis for a new line of business

- Providing services and support to other customers

- Improving your strategy and focus

- Helping you gain a position of thought leadership in the industry

- Providing contacts and access to new sources of valuable information

Unleashing Catie's Hidden Wealth

Catie, as we saw earlier, shows obvious signs of being an outstanding customer advocate and influencer. Not only does she self-identify as a "promoter" of your company in your NPS surveys, but also she's a sophisticated user of social media, and judging by the conversations she generates, her opinions are respected by her peers and those in her extended industry networks—networks that are of high interest to your firm. (In subsequent chapters we'll learn more about the specific behaviors and attitudes that indicate high-potential advocacy.)

Now, instead of *assuming* Catie will engage in promoting your firm, you implement a *system* that maximizes the value customers like her can create. How to actually do so—the various programs and processes you'll need—will be covered in subsequent chapters. For now, we'll see what they result in from the *customer's* experience and point of view.

You may, for example, designate a group—such as a customer reference program—to intentionally reach out and begin building a relationship with Catie and other customers like her. As your team gets to know more about her, ideally in ways that include old-fashioned human-to-human conversations, you learn about her personal and business aspirations and you begin working with her to create a vibrant, reciprocal exchange of value. When you discover that Catie also hopes to expand her entrepreneurial presence in several businesses across her industry that are also relevant to you, you've identified Catie as a potential rock star customer.

In return, Catie reveals that she's quite open to playing an advocacy role for you, based on her personal and professional goals. Note: This is not about crass rewards or bribes to encourage an ambivalent customer to say great things about you. It's about working with customers who are passionate about the value you provide.

As you begin to send Catie new product and industry information—including thought leadership from your internal experts that's relevant to her, her audience, and their businesses—Catie spreads the word through her blogs and tweets. Affirming comments about you increase on the Internet and in the media, and you arrange to produce a video of Catie talking about the important work she's doing, with your help, that's growing her business. Catie touts the video to her network and through posts on her Web site, driving more traffic to your site, and the video becomes one of the most viewed click-ons there. You and Catie go on to create a Webinar that she promotes to her network because, again, the focus isn't on your firm or its products and services but on how her business is succeeding due to smart choices she's made—with your valuable help. The Webinar is a big draw, including new prospects from Catie's network.

As you find and cultivate more customers like Catie, you decide to do more local events to bring such advocates together with prospects and some media people. Catie is quite open to this too, wanting to speak more and build media relationships as well. Those events turn out to be terrific sales vehicles, and, as other companies such as SFDC and Hitachi Data Systems have found, your close rates are significantly higher for prospects who attend the events. You also find, as you survey participants, that what matters most to them is the chance to talk to their peers, confirming that it's customers like Catie who are closing these deals.

As time goes on, you bring Catie and others like her to your annual customer conference, where the same basic dynamic occurs. As with local events, customers and prospects want to speak to each other, and when they do, deals get closed, contracts get renewed, share of wallet increases, and over time, the total amount spent by customers increases.

Meanwhile, your thought-leadership feeds to Catie continue to draw on your knowledge of her industry to show how she can succeed—rather than focusing mainly on your products and services. This leads you to work with Catie to create a presentation for her industry association meetings, which creates substantial interest and yet more new prospects for your firm. She also becomes much more active in your customer communities, commenting, posting, and building her reputation along with awareness of the many offerings and services you provide that even your existing customers weren't aware of.

That information alone would be enough to convince many executives of Catie's value to your firm. But it's not *really* convincing—yet. Some customers engaged in such activities, however energetic and beneficial to your firm they may appear, aren't generating actual profits. She may not actually be bringing in customers. Or she may be bringing in the wrong customers—customers who aren't generating significant revenue or profits. To uncover which customers really are doing so, you need to take the next step. You need to find out and track this information from time to time. (See the sidebar "Customer Value Creation and the 80/20 Rule.")

Customer Value Creation and the 80/20 Rule

Among the great ironies of modern business is that although the prosperity of most firms relies entirely on customers, many firms have no idea of how much real economic value their customers contribute. When they do find out, they're often shocked. Some firms—traditional enterprise software firms provide a good example—learn this when initial rapid growth stalls, sending their stock price into a tailspin. Why? Because the true economic value of the firm's customers is actually quite small or even negative. But that's masked on financial statements by rapidly growing *apparent* profits due to large up-front payments from a fast-growing base of customers. Such "profits," of course, disappear when growth simply slows down a bit, to the shock and consternation of investors.

Other, luckier firms learn they have the problem before their stock price tanks, by performing a relatively easy diagnostic of the true *economic value* of their customers. What they often find is a version of the 80/20 rule (see "Customer value and the 80/20 rule"). Only 10 percent to 20 percent of their customers are contributing significant value to the firm—and they're often not who the firm thinks they are. If companies don't have a good grip on who those 10 percent or 20 percent are, they can wind up wasting millions of dollars on marketing to, pursuing, and servicing the "wrong" 70 percent to 80 percent.

The 80/20 rule appears to apply not only to the value generated by customers from their *purchasing* but also to the *hidden value* they

Capturing the Value Catie Creates

There are essentially five things a customer advocate, influencer, or contributor can do to make an impact on the growth and profitability of your business. He or she can help do the following:

- Acquire customers

- Retain customers

generate—in the form of such things as referrals. That, in a nutshell, is why it's critical to measure customer value.

Customer value and the 80/20 rule

The term *customer value* applies to *all* value generated by customers—including purchasing as well as value generated by referrals, word of mouth, influencer behavior, and contributions to knowledge.

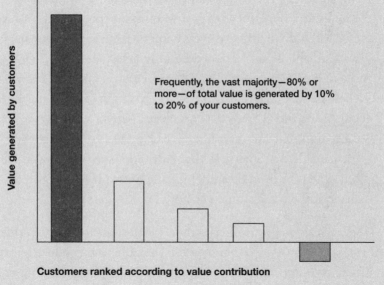

Frequently, the vast majority—80% or more—of total value is generated by 10% to 20% of your customers.

- Increase the company's share of wallet from customers or grow the overall amount the customer spends

- Decrease costs (this includes the cost of acquiring and retaining customers as well as the cost of supplying your products and services)

- Decrease the capital costs associated with customers

When determining how much credit should go to customer AICs for generating profits in these ways, two possibilities exist:

- *Full credit.* In some cases, you can attribute the full profitability generated by a customer to a single advocate or influencer such as Catie. This can happen, for example, when Catie provides a referral who winds up purchasing and says in a post-sale survey that he would not have become a customer if it hadn't been for Catie.

- *Partial credit.* In other cases, Catie gets credit for generating a *part* of the customer's profitability. This can happen when Catie provides a referral who says he purchased because of Catie but would have eventually become a customer anyway, in which case Catie would only get credit for reducing the cost of acquisition. Partial credit is also appropriate when Catie's efforts can't be tied directly to any specific customer, but her advocacy played a significant part in a marketing campaign that did create, retain, or grow sales to a set of identifiable customers. In that case, you score Catie's contribution to the overall campaign, and award her a weighted share of the total profits generated by the campaign.

Here's what you learn when you analyze the data for our hypothetical customer, Catie. As a result of the valuable new-product release and industry information you provided to Catie, her blogging and social media activities drove 12 leads to your Web site and call center during the year. Her Webinar drove another 10 leads. Her outstanding customer video engaged another 12 leads and moved them deeper into the buy cycle. The average close rate for the 34 leads generated by her blogging, social media, and customer video was about 34 percent (figure 2-1), for a total of 12 new customers generated.

Note that Catie doesn't get credit for the profits generated by all 12 buyers. Other marketing and sales factors likely played a role as well, so for each group she's assigned an appropriate "partial credit factor." For the customers generated by her Webinar, who were not already in your database, she gets credit for 100 percent of

FIGURE 2-1

How customer advocates, influencers, and contributors generate economic value

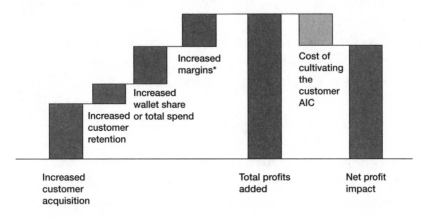

*Customers can increase margins by helping you reduce your costs or reduce the capital required to acquire or serve your customers.

their profits. For the customers generated (in part) by her blogging, social media activities, and customer video, she gets less credit because other factors contributed, such as efforts of the sales team or the use of a broader marketing campaign.

If we take a look at the three types of live events in which she participated—the local events, the annual customer conference, and her professional association meeting, where she did some combination of promoting to her network, speaking, responding to questions, blogging during the event, meeting with prospects, and the like—she received partial credit for five, four, and eight customers, respectively, making 17 more. She was particularly effective in generating customers for you in her presentation at her own professional association.

Because of her growing participation in your advocacy efforts along with her growing reputation and influence, several new customers gave Catie credit for referring them. In particular, three direct-referral customers reported that they would not have otherwise purchased except for Catie, for which she gets 100 percent credit for the profits they generated. Five other customers cited her as their referral source as well, but said they would likely have purchased from you eventually even if Catie had not referred them, so for those Catie gets partial credit (40 percent) for reducing their cost of acquisition.

That's the kind of information you need in order to fully develop the hidden wealth of customers like Catie. I'll conclude this chapter by showing how to do so in a relatively simple way.

Capture the Data

Catie's involvement in the activities described above are easily captured in your customer relationship management (CRM) system, particularly when you have staff dedicated to uncovering and nurturing such advocacy and influencer relationships with customers like Catie.

But remember, the second important piece is to make sure Catie is attracting the *right* customers to your firm—those who generate significant profits. It's critical to look not just at the *revenue* such customers contribute, but also at their *profitability* to your firm. As discussed earlier, a rapidly growing software firm may think it's generating tremendous profits that turn out to be dangerously illusory. Or you may have a few large, high-revenue customers whose demands for price concessions, additional services, or high inventory levels may squeeze margins down to the vanishing point. So you want to make sure Catie is bringing in customers that are not just generating robust revenues but also robust profit margins.

Also recall that we want the data to distinguish between those customers for which Catie gets full credit for bringing them to you and those for which she gets partial credit in situations where she's just a part of an overall marketing campaign. We'll want to assess how *significant* a part she played. A dedicated "hidden wealth-building" staff can provide an educated judgment on what such partial credit should be.

Table 2-1 illustrates how this data can be captured and displayed in your CRM system. In particular, the table shows how the raw

TABLE 2-1

Capturing the data

Customer: Catie

PURCHASING

	Revenue	Profit margin	Profit generated
PROFIT GENERATED BY CATIE	$6,000	40%	$2,400

ADVOCACY AND INFLUENCE	Leads/referrals	Close rate	Acquired customers	Average revenue/customer	Total revenue	Profit margin	Profit generated	Partial credit factor	Profit impact
Leads generated by Catie									
Blog and social media	12	25%	3	$6,000	$18,000	40%	$7,200	60%	$4,320
Webinar	10	50%	5	$6,000	$30,000	50%	$15,000	100%	$15,000
Customer video	12	33%	4	$8,000	$31,680	30%	$9,504	50%	$4,752
Live events									
Local events	8	62%	5	$5,000	$24,800	50%	$12,400	50%	$6,200
Annual customer conference	8	50%	4	$7,500	$30,000	40%	$12,000	40%	$4,800

(continued)

TABLE 2-1 (continued)

ADVOCACY AND INFLUENCE	Leads/ referrals	Close rate	Acquired customers	Average revenue/ customer	Total revenue	Profit margin	Profit generated	Partial credit factor	Profit impact	
Professional association meetings	15	50%	8	$5,500	$41,250	40%	$16,500	80%	$13,200	$48,272
Referrals by Catie										
Direct	4	75%	3	$6,000	$18,000	50%	$9,000	100%	$9,000	
Strongly influenced	7	66%	5	$5,500	$25,410	30%	$7,623	40%	$3,049	$12,049
Totals	76		37		$219,140		$89,227		$60,321	
	Leads/ referrals		Acquired customers		New revenue		Profit generated		Total profit impact	
Cost to support Catie's AIC efforts									–$5,000	–$5,000
Net profit impact generated by Catie										$55,321
ROR (return on relationship)										11.1

figures outlined above measure up in terms of profit impact generated by Catie, based on revenue generated by the new customers she brings in, adjusted by their profit margins, and then adjusted by appropriate partial credit factors for Catie.

Table 2-1 shows in a single glance the scale of the tremendous hidden—and for too many companies, *unrealized*—wealth that customers like Catie can unleash. Catie generated a total of 76 leads, 36 of which became customers generating more than $200,000 in revenue. After adjusting for the profits they generated and appropriate partial credit factors for her, Catie wound up generating $60,321 in profits for the year. Finally, we adjust for the allocated portion of the cost of administering the AIC programs that support customers such as Catie (at $5,000) to arrive at her net profit impact on the company of $55,321. That results in an ROR of 11.1 for Catie. Not bad for a customer whose actual purchases generate only $2,400 in profit per year. By intentionally nurturing her far-greater potential hidden wealth as an advocate and influencer, she's generating 23 times as much in profits from her advocacy and influence as she is from her purchasing.

In the rest of this book, using dozens of case studies, we'll see the tremendous variety of ways in which companies are uncovering and unleashing the hidden wealth of customers like Catie. Let's start in the next chapter with a look at how customers can help you sell your products.

Key Tasks

Using Return on Relationship to Turn Customer Engagement into Organic Growth.

- Recognize that relatively few of your customers—even your most loyal customers—are generating referrals, leads, brand awareness, or other hidden wealth for your firm. You'll need a *system,* including staffing and measurement, to tap into that wealth.

- Staff your hidden-wealth initiatives with people skilled at building high-mutual-value relationships with customers—as opposed to people focused on getting the reference, referral, or lead from your potential advocates, influencers, and contributors.

- Keep key data in your CRM system for your customers' hidden-wealth activities—including leads and referrals generated, partial credit scores, revenue and profit margins contributed from new customers generated, and ROR.

- Just as it's critical to know how profitable your customers are in regard to their purchases, so too it's critical to know how much profitable business your customer AICs are generating.

3

The Most Powerful
Sales Force

Your Customers Are More Credible
to a Buyer Than You Are

BEFORE SHE EVER BEGINS to engage with you, your next customer has already found out everything she needs to know.
She's checked out your products and services on the Web
through an arsenal of communities, blogs, and posts from industry
and media commentators. She has gotten a thumbs up or down on
your business from your customers on her personal network and
social media sites. In other words, she won't even consider talking
to you directly until late in the buying cycle, only *after* she's communicated with her peers.

No wonder traditional sales and marketing pitches fall short
these days in wooing skeptical buyers! Instead, it's customers themselves who are making your sales for you, and they have little in
common with old-school sales and marketing departments. Make
no mistake, it's these very customers—particularly your advocates
and influencers—who can generate substantial ROR for your business. Cultivated and organized in the right way, they'll spread posi-

tive word of mouth, talk directly to prospective buyers, provide highly credible information to analysts and the media, attend and speak at your live events, help build your brand, provide a foundation for your community marketing efforts, help launch your new products, and more.

This new customer value proposition addresses a problem that I've heard executives complain about again and again: the difficulty of finding salespeople who actually *understand* their customers, including the businesses they manage, their very different view of the world and of what matters, and the emotions that keep them awake at night. By bringing more of your customers *into* the sales process, you tap into the easy, mutual understanding that emerges naturally among like-minded souls.

This was precisely the foundation for rapid growth that Marc Benioff established at Salesforce.com, using live events that brought happy customers together with prospective customers. We'll start by taking a look at how he orchestrated these events and how they provided fertile ground for developing effective customer advocates, and then continue the chapter with specific advice for launching customers' advocacy with a successful customer reference program.

How Salesforce.com Built a Business with Customer Salespeople

In chapter 1 we saw how SFDC built a billion-dollar customer relationship management business on a foundation of customer engagement and advocacy. Bringing customers into its sales process through City Tour events required considerable creativity. Let's take a closer look at how this worked.

As we learned earlier, SFDC successfully challenged much bigger, better-funded competitors with a two-pronged approach. First was getting industry publications to write about the upstart firm, with its provocative "The end of software" slogan and No Software logo. That helped attract prospects to the second prong of SFDC's

Tips for Successful Customer Selling Events

- Have events in first-class settings. Despite tight budgets, Benioff and his team learned that it was worth the money to use four- and five-star hotels to project an image of success.

- Keep them short. Many event programs that SFDC thought were essential could be cut or disregarded altogether. Basically, people wanted to interact with their peers and learn just enough about SFDC to know whether it could help them do their jobs.

- Make the event reflect who you are. The image SFDC wanted to project was "innovative." So the events contained a number of creative touches such as sign-in kiosks similar to those used for airport automated check-ins.

- Don't go for quantity—that is, big audiences. Go for quality and mix. In the end, it's about closing deals and generating word of mouth.

- Have a networking reception before the event to facilitate inter-action, as well as afterward to keep the enthusiasm going. This is another reason to keep the formal event short, so that people don't run out of steam.

- Be sure to get customer testimonials *on site.* That way you capture their enthusiasm plus the crowd energy. Then put them on your Web site (with their approval).

- Know what you want attendees to do next, after the event—try a demo, attend a follow-up meeting, whatever—and organize the end-of-event experience to point them in that direction.

- Prep your company team members thoroughly: one bad apple or experience can spoil the whole thing for an attendee.

approach: the local City Tour events in which prospects encountered not regular salespeople but, in effect, customer salespeople.

Note that City Tour events shared certain key features. For one thing, Benioff made sure that his team was well prepared for its presentations, with no embarrassing glitches to mar the customer experience, and he held the events in elegant, top-notch venues. He also kept the programs short to leave plenty of time for interacting and networking. (See the sidebar "Tips for Successful Customer Selling Events" for more guidelines.)

Benioff and his team learned what works and what doesn't in what are, in effect, new types of sales meetings. The results have been exceptional. Prospects who attend the events are more likely than other customer prospects to do the following:

- Buy from SFDC (with an average 80 percent close rate)

- Sign more quickly

- Sign for larger deals

Ultimately, Salesforce.com learned two big lessons from the City Tours: first, the number of attendees is less important than the quality of the mix of people; and second, to leverage customer salespeople, it's crucial to build a customer reference program. Let's look at each of these lessons in turn.

Fortify Your Events with a Powerful Mix of People

Traditionally, CRM industry events *segregate* customers from prospects, which speaks volumes about the problems in the industry that Benioff exploited with such relish. "You don't want customers airing dirty laundry," says chief marketing officer Kendall Collins. "But at our events, we put them all together. We were confident our customers were happy because they were paying month-to-month, making it easy for them to leave and imperative on us to keep them happy."

From the beginning, in addition to prospects and customers, SFDC invited journalists, analysts, and partner firms, along with philanthropists and nonprofit organizations, to City Tour events, creating a stimulating, creative atmosphere. Soon, as Benioff and his team became more proficient at running and capitalizing on the events, they increasingly took themselves out of the limelight. For example, Benioff gave an elaborate keynote address at the first few events. But after a while those gave way to more time for customer interactions—a format that created much more interest. Says Benioff, "Initially we were surprised to find ourselves watching from the sidelines as a group of 60 people suddenly broke into conversation about how to use our service."

SFDC increasingly built in more time and opportunity for such customer–prospect exchanges, with Benioff asking customers from the audience to answer questions or amplify points during his own presentations. These customers, of course, provided more credibility than he ever could, while simultaneously building a base of testimonials for the firm. In addition to creating a new kind of sales environment that prospects loved, the events have also become a kind of marketing laboratory in which customers learn how to speak on behalf of the firm—not by talking to a reporter or in front of a camera, but by talking directly to the firm's market.

Build a Customer Reference Program

A second lesson SFDC garnered from its City Tour events was the importance of establishing a good customer reference program (CRP). The company knew it was creating a small but passionate customer base, and worked to capitalize on this asset. Rather than depend on customers to provide referrals and spread word of mouth on their own, however, Benioff developed a CRP to organize the company's ever-growing number of advocates.

For example, the company CRP team invites area customers to attend City Tour events and solicits stories they might like to tell about using the platform. This preps customers for media interviews, and the best stories often wind up on the event agenda. At the events, the team shoots pictures and video to capture customer experience information and testimonials. Afterward, CRP managers stay in touch with such customers, continue to build the relationships, and encourage interaction between customers and prospects, either on their own or through SFDC blogs, community sites, and other events.[1]

Benioff and his team found that in smaller market cities, they could dispense with a formal program and simply invite local customers, prospects, media, nonprofits, and the like to purely social events—in effect, evening cocktail parties. These gatherings turned out to cost one-tenth of the formal City Tour events—and they provided *the same results:* prospects were as likely to close, and do so as quickly and with the same average (larger) deal size, as those who attended the City Tour events. Which, of course, confirms that the value customers get is entirely from the opportunity to interact in free-flowing conversations with their peers. In the process, SFDC taps value from its customers that goes far beyond their monthly subscription fees.

After these events are over, CRP teams at SFDC follow up by calling on the customer references they garnered—for example, when the company needs a testimonial, a reference call to a prospective customer, or an interview with the press or an analyst. All SFDC marketing materials lead with third-party testimonials, either from analysts or customers, much of it generated at City Tour and other events.

Of course, references are central to the ordinary sales process at SFDC when a buyer wants to talk to a customer. Indeed, Benioff insisted that three of the five steps in all sales calls feature references: provide success stories from customers; verify success stories with customer testimonials; and provide a customer for the prospect to contact.

I'll devote the rest of this chapter to how you can develop your own CRP, starting with a look at what *not* to do.

How to Build an Effective Customer Reference Program

SFDC's approach hinges on getting customers into the sales process and cultivating them for further sales and marketing efforts through an organized CRP. Unfortunately, many firms that attempt to build such reference programs wind up stumbling for reasons that are quite avoidable. This has been especially true over the last decade or so.

Several factors can intrude to undermine what is an increasingly essential sales and marketing tool. Too often company leaders ask, "How can we get more customers to become references for us?" *before* they ensure they're offering great products and services to begin with. Some marketing professionals get caught up in whether they have the right legal agreements or the right approach to inviting customers into a reference program, or whether they're offering the right incentives. "Should we give nice gifts?" they'll ask. "Should we provide training or service discounts?"

Other pitfalls include building a reference pipeline divorced from corporate strategy. Another (and even more surprising) one is not knowing who your happy customers are in the first place. (See the SAP story in the following section, "Uncover Your Existing References.")

In many companies, the CRP is viewed as a junior-staff activity and a cost center. Junior staffers operating a reference program from a spreadsheet will never generate the sort of customer reference value that Salesforce.com, Intel, National Instruments, and others described in this book have been able to do. Tasked with building a pipeline of customer references without strategic direction, junior staffers will naturally look to the following customer groups for references:

- Their biggest revenue customers

- "Marquee" customers

- Customers nominated by the sales department, account management teams, or service teams—people who deal with customers on a regular basis

- Customers nominated by senior executives

- Members of their customer advisory boards or customer councils

- Customers who participate in online communities or forums

Some or all of these groups may provide fertile fields for harvesting customer references, but without strategic guidance and a careful vetting process, they might also prove to be land mines.

For example, your biggest-revenue customers may be exasperated with your offerings and looking desperately for ways to replace you. They may also be in markets from which your firm is strategically moving away. Salespeople who suggest their own clients as references often stop checking in once the sale is closed, and they may be sending you customers who have become disenchanted. Many executives suggest customer reference candidates with whom they simply have a personal relationship, rather than customers who actually have a compelling story about your services. Even customer service teams can sometimes be the last to know of problems with a particular customer relationship. What's more, happy customers may not be *strategic* customers who can provide meaningful recommendations to buyers in the markets you're currently pursuing.

All of this is to say that companies often *think* they know who their customer references are, but in fact are dead wrong (see figure 3-1). Even customers who are currently in your customer reference program may actually turn out to be poor references, as SAP discovered a few years ago.

Let's look now at four keys to building your CRP. In essence: uncover your existing references; create a compelling value proposition; craft a serious business model; and expand your model to support your strategic initiatives.

Uncover Your Existing References

Remember: your references may not be who you think they are. That's what Coleen Kaiser, at the time vice president of customer value and reference service at SAP, found to her astonishment when she took over the firm's global customer reference program. (Keep in mind that SAP is one of the smartest software firms in the world—that should tell you how easily a company can stumble when it comes to developing CRPs.)

FIGURE 3-1

Actual promoters and customer references

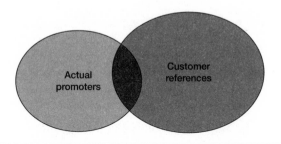

Several business units at SAP had been diligently using Net Promoter Score surveys to determine which of its customers regarded themselves as enthusiastic references. Analyzing that data, along with data from SAP's reference programs, Kaiser found that— remarkably—very few self-identified "promoters" from the surveys were actually in the SAP reference program. This was despite the fact they explicitly told the firm that they would be "very likely" to recommend it to a friend or colleague! All SAP needed to do was ask, but it never had.

At the same time, relatively few of the customers in SAP's reference program—the customers they *were* using as references— identified themselves as promoters in the surveys. That is, SAP's customer references weren't particularly enthusiastic about recommending the firm! Evidently, managers were inviting customers into reference programs based on tips from account executives, personal relationships, or perhaps the "marquee" value of the firm name.

To correct this hit-or-miss system, here's what Coleen did:

- She moved the tepid non-references out of SAP's customer reference programs.

- She moved the promoters in. Whereas previously, fewer than 20 percent of promoters were in the SAP reference program, she shepherded in another 70 percent-plus of the promoters. (It wasn't that hard. Remember, promoters *want* to promote you.)

Soon the reference programs began nudging up the needle on sales. In the after-sale "win-loss" surveys, the importance of references for closing deals went from "neutral" to becoming one of SAP's highest-ranking competitive advantages.

Create a Compelling Value Proposition

The question most firms seem to ask is, "How can we find more customer references?" A better question is, "How do you *create* customer references?" The answer: "Create a great value proposition." Here's how to do so.

- *The starting point (which everyone knows but many firms lose sight of over time): deliver what you promise and promptly fix what goes wrong.* These actions are what generate genuine enthusiasm from a customer, and without that, you don't have a real reference. You can't create or enlist a customer advocate or build a customer-based sales force without the solid foundation of an ongoing, responsive relationship.

- *Know your customers' problems.* "The most important thing you can bring to a dialogue with me is knowing my challenges," says Patty Morrison, CIO of Cardinal Health. "And it's really not that hard." She suggests that reference program managers invest in, or otherwise get access to, their firm's market research about key-customer references. "If you want to develop a customer as a reference, know everything you can about them. And then know everything you can about your important prospects too."

- *Put your customer references together with their peers.* Your firm is in a great position to connect your customers to their peers—other executives and managers like themselves who deal with similar issues. And those connections are highly valued. But where do you find them? Among your other customers, of course. Find ways to bring them together—live, in teleconferences, on the Internet—so that they can exchange ideas and learn from each other. Often, that can be done in the context of events, such as industry conferences, at which they're providing references for you as well.

- *Market and sell your customers.* Tout your *customers'* achievements as much—if not more than—your own in that white paper or case study. Work with your customer's PR firm to align your respective marketing messages.

- *Provide your customer references with opportunities for growth.* Often your most dynamic customer references are eager for personal and professional development. Provide these in the form of speaking opportunities, interviews with the media, and the like, where customers can demonstrate thought leadership.

- *Remember, you have leverage.* If your firm is a smaller supplier or brand new, your customers want to help you. "Helping my smaller vendors grow and get established is in my interest," notes Morrison. "So I'm willing to do what I can to help you grow your customer base. On the other hand, if you're larger and better established, you can help me reward my team by creating opportunities for them to showcase their work at conferences and present papers. It's great career development for them."

- *Tie referencing to performance.* For larger relationship accounts, some reference programs try putting an agreement to provide references up front in the customer's contract—a major and obvious turnoff. Yet many companies persist in doing, or trying to do, this. A better, value-based approach is to initiate a quarterly review process that looks more like the following (notice how providing references evolves naturally):

1. First, review all performance metrics with the customer every three months. Make sure they're being met. If any are not, address the problems swiftly.

2. Next, identify how your solutions are benefiting the customer and then document it. This is a superb win-win that provides customers with verification, a learning tool, and a basis for building best practices, while providing a case study or success story for you.

3. At this point (not before!), with everyone feeling good about the relationship, turn to a discussion of your prospects who are facing similar issues. By now your customer will be ready to open up her contact lists and talk to prospects on your behalf.

- *If possible—and it often is—align your PR messaging with your customer's.* "If you want a customer to speak as a public reference for you," notes Morrison, "you need to understand the message their own PR team is trying to get out to the world about their company. And then ask, how might your message tie into theirs?" When she was CIO at Motorola, for example, the company had public positions on things like mobility, devices, and public safety. So, if you're doing business with Motorola, how can you tie your messaging to theirs? "If my PR person comes into my office with you and you both say, 'Here's the messaging we think benefits both our companies,' then I see a win-win. I'm there."

- *Offer other customer-engagement possibilities.* This is particularly important for your higher-level key customers, who may very well want to provide input into product or solutions development, or even your strategic direction. Offer such customers positions on your advisory boards or executive forums. (We will explore this aspect of ROR in depth in later chapters.) Or they may want to engage with your other customers or other peers in community efforts.

- *Succeed!* A customer who's taken the risk of putting her eggs in your basket *wants* you to succeed for obvious reasons—if yours is a small company, you're more likely to survive. If you're a large firm, you're more likely to invest research and product development dollars improving the solutions you're providing. And that's true even if your customer is a large or even marquee customer. Don't be intimidated about asking for appropriate reference support.

Craft a Serious Business Model That a CFO Will Love

Well-run CRPs can provide substantial value in areas critical to business success: more credible and more effective marketing, improved lead generation, greater sales productivity, higher close rates. But CRPs are expensive. They require staffing; budgets for pricey publishing, video production, and online programs; and, for larger programs, a sophisticated reference management system. In addition, poorly funded reference programs can completely miss tremendous opportunities to generate leads, build brand, and close deals. Indeed, they can wind up alienating the customers they do touch, by overrelying, for example, on their most accommodating customer references until they tick them off.

A proper reference program, therefore, deserves to be run under a proper business model. Here are two suggestions for doing so, based on one particularly outstanding program.

Tie the Reference Program Operations to Corporate Strategy

First, put the reference program directly under a senior executive who has a significant voice in corporate strategy. Consider making the sponsor a sales executive. Often, reference program managers or directors report to marketing executives, but some of the most successful programs I've seen report to sales because that's where they have the most impact. Often firms staff reference programs with people who have sales experience, the better to understand sales needs.

Reference staff should participate in strategic implementations and be kept abreast of strategic planning through their executive sponsor. Reference programs are expensive to staff and operate. In the absence of clear strategic alignment, you'll wind up with customer references who won't matter to strategic prospects, along with expensive collateral, video, and community marketing efforts that buyers won't read or engage with.

Make the Case for a Serious Reference Program

Many, perhaps most, of the senior management in your firm may not be aware of reference programs, what they do, or why they matter. Make no mistake: awareness building and education are essential to get the funding and senior-level support a CRP needs to realize its considerable potential.

One persuasive approach that I've seen for generating awareness and support quickly for a reference program works like this. Everyone in your firm will understand that salespeople need references to close deals and perhaps at other points in the sales cycle as well, depending on your firm's offerings. Finding those references, particularly for larger firms with global reach and complex offerings, isn't easy. In one study by Boulder Logic, for example, it took salespeople between five and seven hours to hunt down references themselves.[2] That's time away from selling. Also note, Boulder Logic didn't address the *quality* of such references—many newer salespeople may simply provide the best of a poor group to choose from, because they lack the contacts or knowledge to access the best available.

Here's how to take that concept and build it into an exceptionally powerful business model for your reference program. If your own salespeople are taking, for example, five to seven hours per hunt for a reference needed to further or close a deal, then it's straightforward to calculate how many hours of selling time your entire sales force is losing in a year. Readily available sales productivity figures should then allow you to turn that into a dollar figure.

For example, one midsized technology firm calculated it was losing 13,000 hours of selling time per year, for a total loss conservatively estimated at $12 million in sales. A properly funded reference program—which delivers the best available reference to the right salesperson at the right time—thus would save the firm that much in lost sales. As we've seen, sales support is just one of a wide variety of business impact benefits a reference program can provide. The same firm also calculated that every dollar spent in providing such a reference program creates $5 in additional sales. It also saves another $2 if you add in the cost of sales salaries and benefits, for a total of $7 in return for each dollar invested.

As a result of such readily available evidence, the firm increased the budget for its global reference program more than 60 percent in 2009—a recession year during which most marketing budgets were slashed. In addition, salespeople themselves took note of the impressive data. The number of the firm's top salespeople who make regular use of the reference program went from about one-third to 80 percent in 2009.

Expand Your Model to Support Strategic Initiatives

Armed with such information, reference programs can demonstrate critical contributions to strategic initiatives. When a firm is developing strategies for selling critical new offerings into specific markets, for example, it should include the manager of the reference program in the planning. His presence is a rather obvious step: perhaps the most important marketing tool needed to sell into new markets isn't advertising or PR, but satisfied customers willing to provide referrals to their peers with similar business problems.

Once sales goals are established and formalized for a new offering at the firm mentioned earlier, the reference director can tell his colleagues on the planning board how many reference requests the sales department will make in order to fulfill those goals (information based on the data he's developed over a period of two years). After determining how many references the company will need to cultivate for the new solution, he can quantify the headcount and budget he'll need to support the sales goal, rather than waiting and scrambling for references when the solution reaches the market.

In other words, planners can be assured that if the new product or solution meets customer needs and expectations, its launch won't founder because your most powerful salespeople—your customer references—aren't in place. It's an emotionally powerful value proposition. New product launches are scary things. A lot of things can go wrong. Imagine the comfort that the responsible executives feel in the assurance that they'll (1) have the customer references they need—which are critical to new product success—and (2) keep their salespeople in front of customers rather than wasting time hunting down those references themselves.

As the experience and success of firms like Salesforce.com demonstrate, the customer reference relationship is fundamental to a successful business. In the next few chapters, I'll show how customer advocates and influencers can help you take advantage of advances and opportunities created by social media and community marketing, allowing advocates to advance from sometimes passive roles as references into far more active initiatives—ones that generate much higher economic value added.

Let's turn now to how you can develop customers who will help drive your marketing strategy.

Key Tasks

Engaging Customer Advocates to Help Sell Your Offerings.

- Place customer advocates in a position to sell by interacting with prospects—particularly at live events.

- Form your most promising advocates into a customer reference program that offers them advocacy efforts they enjoy and that in turn creates significant value for your firm.

- Keep your customer reference pipeline full with a strong mutual value proposition, not cheesy incentives or rewards.

- Build your CRP on a sound financial footing, arm it with active senior-level support, and align it with your business strategy.

- Tie reference requests to your firm's performance, review this regularly through surveys or in-person meetings, tout what's working, and fix what isn't. This will avoid reference burnout.

4

The New Marketing Machine

How Customer Advocates Can Drive Marketing Strategy

WANTED: A MODERN APPROACH to marketing your products and services. Many buyers today have mostly made up their minds about you before they ever engage with your sales or marketing efforts. How then do you establish connections with buyers who increasingly rely on others to make up their minds? As we know, they're often turning to anyone *but* you—their friends or colleagues, their expanding social media networks and other sources such as bloggers, independent communities of their peers, and content aggregators, as well as traditional outside venues such as analysts and industry media.

This applies *not just* to your existing markets. As companies expand their reach into new markets or new global regions, the problem is compounded because they have no presence, don't speak the language, and typically have limited marketing budgets. The upshot? Your business is losing customers even though the solutions you're seeking are right in front of you, in your products and services.

By including customer advocates in your marketing efforts, and in particular in the conversations you're having with your market, you can meet these challenges. Organizing and deploying such a marketing communications strategy starts by rethinking your approach in terms of the *opportunities* this new world is creating—which are considerable for companies who become skilled at engaging with their customers to get the word out.

Effective ways to frame your approach to marketing include creating "marketing gravity," accelerating customer engagement, and becoming an industry thought leader. In this chapter we will explore each of these steps, as well as examining companies that are already doing these things, such as Hitachi Data Systems, Eloqua, Microsoft, and SAS Institute (Canada). Let's begin with the first step—grooming your customer advocates to attract new customers.

Create Marketing Gravity

More useful than a "push-pull" approach to marketing communications, which suggests some sort of wrestling match, is an "attraction" strategy, which can be formulated as *marketing gravity*—a concept developed by über-consultant Alan Weiss and his community of individual and small-firm management consultants.[1] His group is as effective as any I've encountered at establishing and building long-term relationships with key customers.

For our purposes we'll adapt Weiss's concept to illustrate how your *customers* can help you establish and build those relationships. The idea is to build a picture of how marketing communication looks for your firm in today's world of easy access to information and two-way conversations, and then see where your customer advocates can enhance your firm's gravitational pull.

For example, figure 4-1 depicts a B2B firm that provides products and services. This one illustrates just a few of the possibilities—I've seen one marketing gravity chart that contained more than 130 "gravitational pull" items.

FIGURE 4-1

Marketing gravity

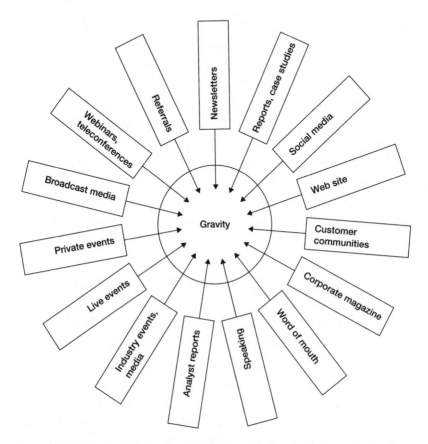

Source: Adapted from Alan Weiss, *The Consulting Bible: Everything You Need to Know to Create and Expand a Seven-Figure Consulting Practice* (Hoboken, NJ: Wiley, 2011).

Using this chart as a guide, you can identify individual gravitational pull based on your business and industry. Then think through how customers in your market access information and conversations about your industry, or how they might be open to being engaged.

That bears repeating: *be sure to look specifically for ways to bring customer advocates into marketing gravity.* As you can see, they can play important roles in most, if not all, of these attraction tools. You can interview them in your newsletters or company magazine, feature their experiences in teleconferences, and promote them to media outlets or industry analysts (which place high value on customer experiences when reporting about product releases or industry trends). Customer videos are exceptionally powerful tools for engaging buyers, as we'll see in chapter 5, even in early product marketing campaigns such as beta or early adopter programs.

Unleashing this peer information and dialogue into your market in a timely, high-impact fashion requires an organized and systematic effort—not unlike a modern media company—within your own company. The following section focuses on the second step of the process, which will help you select and prioritize marketing gravity efforts in a way that maximizes their attraction.

Accelerating Customer Engagement

The second step for launching an attraction approach to marketing is the accelerant curve (figure 4-2).[2] This useful framework helps you to think about how you can accelerate the creation of mutual, high-value engagement with key customers.

In the accelerant curve, you combine effective, staged aspects of your marketing gravity plan with your value proposition. The idea is not to regard all marketing gravity efforts as equal in value, but over time to determine which will make it easiest and most compelling for prospects to engage with your firm, and then accelerate the process of moving them rapidly from the initial education stage (on the left of the curve) to the most intimate and profitable exchange of high mutual value (on the right).

For customers who don't know you, you start at the left, making it easy to engage with you with three or four inexpensive or free offerings. As you progress to the right, you're providing more value (from demos to introductory products or services to more comprehensive products and services) and, often, more intimacy

FIGURE 4-2

The accelerant curve

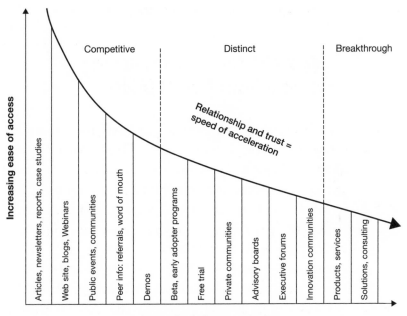

Source: Adapted from Alan Weiss, *The Consulting Bible: Everything You Need to Know to Create and Expand a Seven-Figure Consulting Practice* (Hoboken, NJ: Wiley, 2011).

(personal service, access to rapid response, access to advisory boards or executive forums and the like). Note that the key accelerator is *trust*—which naturally evolves through this incremental staging of your engagement with the customer.

If it is particularly effective, your accelerant strategy has "leaps," or stages of engagement so effective that the prospect jumps or leaps directly to the most intimate and lucrative stage of engagement at the far right after having interacted with you in only one or two initial stages.

These constructs, marketing gravity plus the accelerant curve, are exceptionally versatile. They can be used to penetrate new markets, penetrate a single large customer more deeply, or *re*engage existing customers who are drifting away. But to really ratchet up your appeal to customer advocate-marketers, consider how you can become a guru of sorts in your own industry.

Be the Influencer: How to Become an Industry Thought Leader

Influencer marketing—finding and engaging with the influencers, mavens, connectors, network hubs, and the like in your marketplace and getting them to say positive things about you—is now just the ante-up in the current media-saturated environment. The Web has created a platform in which bloggers unaffiliated with traditional media or analyst firms can create large followings that are quite attractive to marketers. Many companies make it a major priority to reach out to them.

What never seems to occur to companies, however, is that *they* are the ones who should be the influencers and thought leaders. Think about it: your own firm probably has access to customers who are in the trenches every day, facing and solving (hopefully with your help) the real-world issues confronting your industry. In addition, your firm has professional business, technical, and process experts who are working side by side with your customers to help them find solutions.

This is the sort of information that outside influencers such as analysts and industry media crave. And you have it. Why depend on a marketing communications strategy that feeds such powerful intellectual property to mediators? Why not *be* the influencer yourself?

If you have your act together—if you have customers who are achieving great things with your help and are passionate about your services, and your experts are among the best in the industry (and these are the price of admission in many industries)—then you're well positioned to become a thought leader. Although

Is Your Company a Thought Leader?

- Your firm constantly disseminates powerful intellectual property (IP) that focuses not on your offerings but on the important issues in the industry.
- Your IP suggests approaches—solutions to such issues that might come from anywhere—not just your firm's products and services.
- Your primary sources are great customers or clients and a tremendous track record—but you're not limited to those.
- Unlike many others in your industry, you're able to make complex topics simple, free of jargon, pragmatic, and always with clear business outcomes in view.
- You're able to make the implicit explicit. For example, you can tease out underlying assumptions widely held in your industry that might be leading people astray.
- You can also make the explicit implicit. That is, your IP provides guidance and actual examples of how practitioners in the real world can take great ideas and incorporate them so thoroughly into their firm that it becomes implicit knowledge, or second nature.
- You're in the public eye. Over time you are looked to as a major authority—if not *the* authority—in your field.
- You're able to change others' perspective—and sometimes change the conversation—in your industry.
- You build your own substantial following and audience. Your IP is quoted and cited frequently by the media because they can't ignore you.
- No one doing business in your industry can afford *not* to listen to you. They may not agree with you and may not use your products and services, but if they ignore you, then they aren't taken seriously by their peers.
- You grow a substantial body of work containing proprietary material, over time.
- You coin phrases cited by others.

there's nothing wrong with developing good relationships with outside influencers or the media, why depend on the kindness of strangers?

Before I describe how one company, Eloqua, became a thought leader, let's take a moment to look at what being a thought leader actually entails. Companies that manage to assume such pundit status in their industries generate a regular, steady stream of high-value intellectual capital (using customers and clients with great track records as primary sources). But they also make sure that the intellectual property they disseminate focuses on critical industry issues—not the company's own offerings. The sidebar "Is Your Company a Thought Leader?" summarizes these and other ways that companies foster thought leadership in their industries.

Eloqua's Markie Awards: Fast Track to Thought Leadership

Eloqua, the marketing intelligence and demand generation firm, is emerging as an important thought leader in its rapid-growth but highly competitive market. As chief technology officer Steve Woods points out, one key is that the firm showcases its customers, their knowledge, and their experience. The vehicle is its well-publicized Markie Awards.

Every year since 2006, Eloqua has hosted the black-tie event for its customers and others in the industry, providing a strong foundation for building its position of thought leadership. These events are a big deal, with awards given out in some twenty categories. The statues that award winners receive were designed by the same firm that designed the Emmy Awards. "We decided that if we were going to do this, we'd do it right," says Woods. An industry panel selects winners representing the best of the best in the industry—whether they are Eloqua customers or not.

"We take pains to make sure that our winners really are the best and that people understand in-depth *why* they won," says Woods. And that's the key to the powerful thought leadership mojo the

Markies create for Eloqua. Not surprisingly, the Markies draw significant media attention.

Eloqua also develops industry-leading best practices in marketing, collected from dozens of winners and finalists—some of which are its customers, many of which are not. Its most successful marketing campaigns in 2009, in fact, were thought leadership pieces based on knowledge gleaned from award winners. For example, Eloqua issued a vendor-neutral, highly successful *Social Media Playbook* that captured information about how its clients and other leading users of social media use those tools. The *Playbook* offers clear, pragmatic information about the use of such tools as Facebook, LinkedIn, and Twitter. This was not promotional material, but pragmatic, useful, and easy-to-understand information that cut through the clutter and confusion of how social media works for marketing executives struggling to make sense of it all.

Meanwhile, a second highly successful thought leadership effort, Eloqua's Infographic campaign, provided an additional tool—a social media content "grid"—that marketers can use to think through and plan their own efforts in new media.

Such campaigns were tremendous successes for Eloqua. Both created large spikes in traffic to its sites—and those numbers carried through to generate proportionally large spikes in revenue.

These, then, are the building blocks of a customer-driven marketing strategy in today's world: (1) establish your company's attraction with marketing gravity, (2) apply an engagement-accelerant curve that fits your business and market, and (3) establish thought leadership. Throughout each of these steps, emphasize content from your customers.

The following sections set forth examples of how three firms—Hitachi Data Systems, Microsoft, and SAS Institute (Canada)—are successfully using some combination of this three-pronged approach to get the word out about their offerings (and the passionate customers they've won as a result) to penetrate new markets and to restore lagging customer retention rates.

Hitachi Data Systems: Moving from Best-Kept Secret to Top of Mind

A few years ago, data storage solutions provider Hitachi Data Systems (HDS) faced a problem. As Brian Householder, senior vice president of worldwide marketing and business development, put it, "We have many passionate customers. But no one in our industry knew about it." The team lacked the presence of larger, older, and better-funded rival EMC.

To tackle the problem, Householder and his team addressed a number of critical issues involving the firm's brand. The team had learned that, in their communication with customers, HDS employees in sales, marketing, and other areas were describing some thirty different versions of the firm's brand to customers! Obviously they needed to get on the same page. Also, in thinking about the sort of brand conversations they wanted to have in their marketplace, Householder and his team needed to decide what specifically they wanted to achieve in the company's new branding effort, what HDS should talk about to get there, and how the firm would get the message out. Needless to say, HDS's passionate customers would play critical roles in finding the answers to these problems.

What follows are lessons gleaned from the steps that HDS ultimately took to rapidly build its market presence.

Start with a Consistent Brand Message That Addresses What's on Customers' Minds

HDS began by developing a single consistent brand message, which became "Data drives our world. Information is the new currency"—a clear appeal to the growing realization in the C suite that technology is playing an increasingly strategic role and can differentiate a firm. HDS placed adherence to the brand message into the firm's MBOs (management by objectives). "If we can't outspend our competition, at least we can make sure we're all saying the same thing," says Asim Zaheer, vice president of corporate and global marketing. In its efforts to get the message into its marketplace, HDS established a goal: gain mindshare in the C suite at large enterprises. "To do this, we needed to make sure that our content was interesting, different, engaging, and provided immediate value to readers," says Zaheer. "And above all, not just another sales pitch."

Here's how they proceeded.

Develop Content That Provides Solutions and Shows You Can Provide More

HDS invested considerable time into thinking through what key issues were on its customers' minds. For example, in 2010, costs were a big factor for CIOs. "So we provided them with information to help them reduce costs," says Zaheer. "The message that we project is, 'We're not just a vendor. We're a business partner.'"

Place Your Internal Experts Front and Center

HDS placed Hu Yoshida, its well-respected chief technology officer, in the limelight to attract high-level audiences. With a blog that showcases his expertise, Yoshida gives C-level readers insights into current trends in topics such as private-cloud computing, virtualization, storage management, and other issues critical to the intended audience. His focus is on helping them think through important issues, not on touting HDS solutions. Unsurprisingly, his blog is attracting audiences in significant numbers. Yoshida brings two advantages that no journalist, blogger, or other outside influencer can match—deep expertise (that's how he got his job with HDS) plus regular, direct access to customers and their issues. These provide a powerful basis for assuming a position of thought leadership.

Execute a Theme-Based Communications Strategy That Emphasizes Customer Stories

Zaheer and his team made a conscious decision to take a thematic approach in their communications. "We didn't want to do one-shot posts or white papers, but instead to develop themes so we could create ongoing conversations." The themes they picked were, again, top of mind to the CIOs, CFOs, and executives running operations that they wanted to reach. "We want readers to get the message that HDS is thinking holistically about solutions to their issues, and not just selling our stuff," says Zaheer.

Important in all HDS thought leadership efforts are customer stories. "If our audience is a bank CFO, we'll talk about a large bank on Wall Street that tackled the issue we're addressing, and how it did so," says Zaheer. What's more, the firm kept customers closely engaged as it rolled out its content, keeping them informed, getting their input and feedback, featuring their stories, and putting them on stage at its live events (more on this in a moment). For customers and prospects who were located where HDS didn't have a presence, the firm took a variety of new and old media steps to rectify that situation.

Like Salesforce.com, which engages with the forgotten end user, Zaheer and his team also wanted to consciously penetrate deeper into the organizations of the customers they wanted to attract. In addition to developing communications that C-level executives will want to read, HDS continues to "go deep" into current issues to attract the more technical people (who will be implementing and living with HDS solutions), to create credibility with them as well.

To Reach Customers, Find Out Where They Are

Zaheer and his team also spent time thinking through how to get the intellectual property HDS developed to its intended audience. One obvious step was to ensure that HDS blogs and other content show up high in Google rankings of the terms that HDS prospects are searching on, such as "storage virtualization." That was achieved first and foremost by having a highly respected CIO putting out exceptionally valuable content.

And because HDS knew that its customers and potential customers communicated on Facebook and Twitter, the firm established a presence in these places with a "facebook.com/HitachiData Systems" page and an "HDScorp" Twitter account, respectively. Unlike many such corporate "social network" pages that fall into the trap of being "all about us," HDS addressed issues it knew its customers were facing. For example, the Facebook page might post a link to "What will be the top tech trends in 2011?"—a blog post by Yoshida. Or it might link networkers to an e-book describing the "Big Five Benefits" of installing a "one file and content storage family" for firms thinking of making that transition. Tweets might include a link to an article on how much money you could save in your data center.

HDS also syndicates content through popular publications and content aggregation sites that reach its intended audience, such as CIO.com, TechTarget.com, and Searchstorage.com. Still, where appropriate, HDS uses traditional marketing outreach channels such as telemarketing, targeted mail, and e-mail lists to disseminate its ideas and promote events that it hosts.

"We're also engaging with influencers in the blogging community," says Zaheer. "Most of them are technical, so we flew a dozen top bloggers in for a 'geek day' at our headquarters." HDS takes what it calls an "open kimono" approach with such bloggers, allowing them to play with the firm's technology to their hearts' content and to talk directly with top HDS officials.

Leverage the Power of Live Events

Like Salesforce.com, HDS found that live events are exceptionally powerful marketing tools. The firm started aggressively, with some forty seminars in major cities around the world, under its revitalized brand theme "Data drives our world. Information is the new currency."

When HDS launched the seminar series in Santa Clara, California, in 2010, Zaheer and his team expected perhaps 150 or so attendees. But 300 showed up, attracted to the firm's growing thought leadership already established on the Web and other channels. They also came because HDS customers (that is, peers of the audience) were on the agenda. In addition, the events included HDS partner firms such as VMware, Brocade, and Cisco—which further emphasized that, rather than a vendor sales pitch, attendees were going to get a comprehensive view of solutions to their issues from their peers.

Subsequent seminars have attracted on average between 150 and 200 attendees per city—and more than one thousand in some global market cities. The mix of attendees is typically twenty or so customers, along with thirty prospective customers at the VP level and above, who are also invited to bring along their teams.

As for costs and outcomes, the good news is that live events are relatively inexpensive on a per-attendee basis. HDS reckons the cost at around $275 per head. The results are more than worth it. In less than two years, 13,000 attendees have participated. HDS is closing on average $1 million in new business with new accounts at each event (not including add-on business with existing accounts).

Also, when HDS puts out major "product refreshes" to keep a product line abreast of evolving customer needs, acceptance has substantially improved as a result of the firm's new approach to marketing. Previously, HDS suffered a serious dip in revenue for the product line that could reach into the hundreds of millions of dollars. "But by reaching out to our audience like we've done in the information seminars and other thought leadership efforts, we're managing to avoid that dip," says Zaheer.

Next we'll look at Microsoft and how it leverages a customer-advocate marketing approach to expand its global presence.

Microsoft: Penetrating and Gaining Market Share Where You Don't Speak the Language

A major challenge for any company is to enter new markets, which often have different customs and norms, along with their own language and ways of communicating. This is particularly true for companies striving to expand into global markets, and it can be an expensive and time- and labor-intensive proposition.

Just ask Microsoft. Even with its piles of cash, the software giant had to get creative when it came to attracting customers in new global markets. That's why Microsoft developed its Most Valuable Professional (MVP) program to tap into an important opportunity: local markets have their own pundits and influencers. These are people who are knowledgeable about the industry, are relatively easy to find, and are known by and can influence others in the market to consider new solutions. Microsoft wanted to find and engage them.

Originally developed to help customers provide product support for each other and recognize and reward those who had been particularly helpful (as well as cut its own support costs), the Microsoft MVP program has since evolved into a full-fledged and scalable marketing gravity generator for the firm, particularly in new markets. The idea is to locate and reward top influencers and technology-community leaders in these markets—who might be thought of as "customers plus"—and begin to engage them in appropriate ways to help inform the market about what Microsoft products can do.

A Few Influencers, a Big Impact

Today, Microsoft has identified and groomed about four thousand MVPs in ninety countries covering about one hundred technologies and some forty languages. This is a tiny number compared with Microsoft's customer base, but they create a substantial impact. Note the thought leadership traits that the MVPs, working with Microsoft, exhibit:

- Local MVPs speak the local language and understand local norms—and eventually they teach Microsoft the same.

- MVPs are far more willing than the average buyer to share relevant Microsoft news and information about offerings to local technical communities, neighbors, and friends.

- They provide exceptional input and actionable feedback on what the market needs and expects from Microsoft products.

- They provide a superb cohort of beta testers for new features and products. "MVP participants account for less than 1 percent of all the beta testers, but they find 27 percent of the bugs that need to get fixed," says Nestor Portillo, who runs the MVP program.

- MVPs provide more than 20 percent of the content—such as white papers, Webcasts, and the like—on Microsoft's Web sites and forums, which are the major technical resource and content destinations for Microsoft developers, information technology (IT) professionals, and consumers. That means that Microsoft's far-flung technical communities have access to critical information helping them to create software and implement solutions for customers in global markets.

Each of these has an impact on Microsoft's bottom line. Yet Portillo is quick to point out that it's not about the amount of money immediately saved or generated by these efforts. "It's about sending the right message: we're helping MVPs help their communities, in their own way, using their own language. And we're helping the MVPs grow their own reputations. Ultimately, it's about getting the right content to our customers." (Note that Portillo touches here on the concept of communities. I call this *community marketing* and will cover it in depth in chapter 6.)

Finding and Cultivating MVP Influencers

Here's how Microsoft develops MVPs for marketing on the front lines.

Define MVP Criteria

Particularly in newer markets with unfamiliar cultures and where your company might not be well known to the population, you can't rely solely on your company's own content and on customer references from home markets to create gravity. You need the right locals. Portillo and his team find them by looking for people who are highly technically adept—often in creative ways—with the

Microsoft product in question. In addition, they have a considerable span of influence.

Specific criteria for choosing a Microsoft MPV include community leaders that are

- Available and easy to access

- Independent

- Deeply knowledgeable about the technology in question

- Able to help others

- Very professional in their interactions with peers

- Able to speak the local language and understand the local ways of disseminating knowledge in nontechnical language

Embrace an Expanded Concept of Advocacy

Microsoft MVPs need not be customer references or even customers who might be particularly willing to recommend Microsoft—which is particularly noteworthy. Microsoft is not just looking for "raving fans" but rather for prominent influencers who will give Microsoft products a fair hearing. "We just require that our MVPs are at least neutral in their attitudes toward Microsoft," says Portillo. Obviously, local Microsoft customers are often candidates for MVP status—but the program also welcomes those who aren't customers but might be at some point.[3] This illustrates a more advanced and more credible concept of advocacy in our increasingly transparent world.

Find Your MVPs, and Let Them Find You

Portillo and his team use a variety of approaches:

- *Listen.* Portillo's team monitors communities in important markets around the world. "Technology is making it increasingly easy to find and monitor conversations and interactions in communities. And it's a high priority for us to continue to improve our listening capabilities." As Microsoft becomes increasingly adept at monitoring community interactions through social media sites or other local media, it becomes pretty clear who the influencers are.

- *Develop good listening tools.* Listening tools such as Jive Market Engagement or Radian 6 are becoming increasingly good at letting Microsoft know how wide a span an MVP candidate has. These tools keep track of how many forums he or she participates in, what is the message and tone conveyed relative to Microsoft and its competitors, and how much commentary and other engagement the candidate receives.

- *Embrace self-nominations.* MVP candidates, by their nature, are frequently not shy about letting you know who they are. MVPs include independent consultants, academics, big corporation employees, small business owners, doctors and lawyers, and more. "One of our top Excel MVPs is a firefighter in Osaka, Japan," says Portillo.

- *Encourage referrals.* A prime source for referrals are other MVPs (influencers tend to know who other influencers are), industry events or conventions (Portillo and his team look particularly for recurring keynote and other speakers), and internal Microsoft employees, particularly those working in the local market.

- *Mine user groups.* This can be accomplished online or in person. For example, says Portillo, "In certain parts of Latin America or Southeast Asia, it's difficult to get Internet access—so user communities will meet live. We'll support those meetings with resources, and often wind up with exceptional MVP candidates."

MVPs can be widely followed bloggers or people who are active on forums or relevant social media sites such as Facebook or LinkedIn. They can include industry speakers, authors, and third-party Web site owners. "'Mr. Excel' runs a Web site that sometimes gets more traffic than our own Excel page," notes Portillo. "Now there's an MVP candidate!"

The ways in which customers can help a firm increase marketing gravity and help move new buyers through the accelerant curve are limited only by a firm's creativity and its ability to truly listen and learn.

Let's look now at how SAS fosters customer advocates in its marketing efforts.

SAS Institute (Canada): Engaging Customer Advocates to Retain Existing Customers

SAS Institute (Canada), Inc., the Canadian subsidiary of the highly respected SAS Institute, found itself with a daunting problem a few years ago. The firm had enjoyed robust retention rates—in the high nineties—for years, but those had fallen to the mid- to high eighties in the early 2000s.

Wally Thiessen, who leads SAS Canada's customer engagement programs, worked with a small marketing team to turn this around. "As we looked more closely at the problem, we discovered a knowledge gap: our customers often weren't aware of important solutions that our software could provide them. We realized that we weren't engaged enough with them."

Here is what SAS Canada did to improve customer engagement—and retention.

Recruit Customer Champions to Build Learning Environments

The idea was to bring key customers, which SAS Canada styled as *champions* and *super champions,* together with other customers and SAS experts into a sharing and learning environment that would attract more and more customers. That combination allowed Thiessen and his team to narrow the knowledge gap and help address issues that SAS Canada customers were having, as well as to generate substantial marketing gravity to change their and the market's declining perception of the value of SAS solutions.

Give Customer Champions Leadership and Organizational Roles

SAS Canada had a few user groups at the time, but they weren't particularly dynamic or well organized. Thiessen and his team started by forming executive committees of local key customers selected from the user groups in thirteen major cities throughout Canada, and worked with them to hold two customer forums each year in their respective cities. The committees helped develop agendas and located speakers (other SAS customers or SAS experts) who would appeal to their audience, and afterward shared best practices that emerged. In addition, they worked with executive committees in the largest cities to conduct other specialty forums on various subjects of interest.

For its largest customers, SAS Canada created a key account program so that Thiessen and his team could work with these customers one on one. It also designated as customer "champions" those who participated in or contributed to these efforts. "Super champions" were those who participated in more than one program. In addition, Thiessen's team launched an e-newsletter.

What motivates the champions to do things such as serving on an executive committee to help run customer events? SAS's best customers cited the following reasons:

- To develop peer relationships

- To achieve industry recognition

- To gain the opportunity to share their success with others

- To improve their personal development

These customers and forums became the tools for a powerful marketing gravity effort. Thiessen's team has developed and leveraged 275 champions and nearly 50 super champions. The customer forums they help to organize draw more than two thousand customers and prospects per year. The e-newsletter has more than five thousand subscribers. Between events, champions keep the conversation going with lively online forums, including an SAS wiki and pages on Facebook, LinkedIn, and other sites.

Focus Events and Content on Customer Issues

SAS Canada has found that specialty forums on topics ranging from data mining to health care to management have a greater impact on increasing demand generation than standard user meetings. "That's because they're specific and focus on topics that attendees are hungry to learn more about," says Thiessen. "For example, our Data Mining Forum focuses on how to apply data mining techniques and approaches to address business challenges—not about SAS software usage." Attendees learn from SAS customers *as well as noncustomer practitioners*—which reinforces that SAS is not conducting a sales pitch. But as it turns out, the meeting is held at SAS, most attendees use SAS, and many presentations refer to SAS to reinforce the company's dominance in this market space.

Thiessen's team takes the same approach with its *Insights* newsletters, which provide information not just on SAS usage but also about conferences, Webinars, and other events in the SAS community.

Find Ways to Cut Costs (Customers Can Help)

Managing these initiatives isn't expensive. Thiessen and a team of just three people manage to oversee all this activity—involving SAS Canada's three hundred prime customer businesses—on a limited budget. Here are some ways in which they save money:

- Speakers at the customer forums are often local—which appeals to audiences who want to learn from peers with whom they can build relationships.

- SAS experts who do travel to speak at the forums also attend client or prospect meetings while in the city.

- Customer executive committees do much of the groundwork for producing and managing the forums; Thiessen's team supports those efforts.

- A well-designed online communication management system saves SAS staff the time it would take to talk directly to the executive committees every time a general message needs to go out.

- Forums are often held at customer sites or universities to save room rental and audiovisual costs.

The upshot for SAS? This closer, more personal engagement between SAS Canada and customers, and among customers themselves, was key to solving the company's retention problem, which climbed back to the high nineties by 2007. Customers who weren't getting what they needed from their SAS software realized they weren't alone, and that they had a peer community to draw on for support. They also learned about capabilities in their software they weren't aware of, which enhanced its value to them.

The champions and super champions, who served on executive committees, were key to this turnaround. "Partnering with individual customers in a host of different ways strengthens ties and stickiness to our software," Thiessen says. "Without these champions, it would be impossible to have the ties we've developed with our customer base."

SAS has found too that the company's customer engagement efforts provide powerful attraction to SAS Canada's market *outside* its customer base. SAS Canada champions and super champions, along with presenters and panelists who participate in the forums or are interviewed in the customer e-newsletter, begin learning how to articulate the value of SAS solutions. They become natural candidates for customer references and public customer advocates.

Marketing's New Role: Engagement Throughout the Customer Life Cycle

Marketing's traditional role in demand generation ends when it hands over a qualified lead to sales, or so it is generally thought. But that approach creates far too limited a view of the impact the marketing department can have on the business by continuing to engage with customers *after* they buy. In fact, the decision to purchase should be just the *warm-up* when it comes to marketing's engagement with the customer. (See figures 4-3 and 4-4.)

The following subsection examines ways to extend marketing's relationship with buyers.

Turn Buyers into Passionate Advocates

Delivery, support, and services, working with the marketing department, try to take key customers (strategic or otherwise highly valued) through an agreed-upon progression, through which the customer becomes:

FIGURE 4-3

Marketing's traditional relationship to the customer stops when he or she buys

Marketing gravity attracts buyers

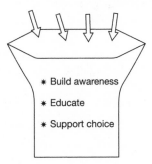

* Build awareness
* Educate
* Support choice

FIGURE 4-4

Marketing's new role: engagement throughout the customer life cycle

Properly engaged buyers can turn into customer advocates, influencers, and contributors, thus dramatically increasing marketing gravity.

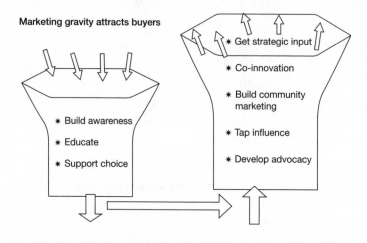

- *Satisfied:* The solution works acceptably well.

- *Retained:* The start of a long-term relationship, but not necessarily loyal, because there may be no acceptable alternatives available.

- *Loyal:* But perhaps with a limited scope of services.

- *A promoter:* Very willing to recommend your firm to a colleague or friend.

- *A trusted adviser (mutual relationship):* Customer and vendor work together to improve and expand scores of services.

- *A trusted partner (mutual relationship):* Relationships graduate to the C level, and these customers are open to the vendor offering solutions for *any* item on the customer's agenda.

As key customers progress through these stages, their value extends well beyond what they purchase: they become exceptionally valuable contributors to your marketing gravity efforts (and the ways in which they can do so are limited only by a company's creativity). What's more, these advocates, when properly engaged, *increase* their loyalty as purchasing customers.

For example, in the early stages of the relationship (even before they buy), customers may be willing to participate in a community that contains your other customers. At some point when you've proven that you're going to provide value, they may be willing to provide references to help the sales department close deals. Later they may be willing to give you a testimonial. As your value and relationship grow, they may be willing to shoot a video and begin to open up their network to provide referrals to their peers whom they think you can help.

As your mutual success continues, and the value you provide becomes tangible, they may be willing to create with you a more detailed case study of their company's lessons learned with your product. Or speak to an audience at industry events about, among other topics, the role you played in their success. Or they might contribute to your newsletter or blog or agree to interviews with the media.

As time goes on, they may agree to serve on your advisory boards, providing you with insights into their future needs and those of the marketplace. As the relationships go up the hierarchy at your key-customer accounts, C-level customers might do many of the above activities as well as serve on executive boards that provide invaluable information that guides your strategy.

All these, in a phrase, are the ingredients for building exceptional marketing gravity and accelerating customer trust, intimacy, and value creation. What kind of value? Your key customers will experience, among other benefits:

- Improved delivery and service

- Better innovation and more strategic solutions over time

- Access to peer interaction and relationships, by participating in your communities, boards, conferences, and the like

- Personal and professional recognition: speaking at industry events, being quoted in media, and so on

These are just a few of the benefits customer advocates will see and experience. But you can look for ways to provide even more. For example, if you're a large enterprise, you have the resources to reward the customer's team with complementary tickets to conferences and other networking and learning experiences. And if you're a small new firm, just *surviving* is a benefit to your customers. That alone makes it more likely that they'll refer business to you.

Properly understood, the threats that marketing faces in today's world—where customers check you out long before they'll talk to you, and in which customers barely understand the increasingly complex solutions you sell—represent superb opportunities. For many firms, the door is wide open to rise above the din to a position of thought leadership in their industry and penetrate global markets, to learn the skills they'll need to engage customers and the people who influence them, and to harvest reams of valuable intelligence and turn it into knowledge.

None of this is simple to do. But companies who work to pursue customer-advocate marketing venues will differentiate themselves far beyond the competition. In the next chapter, we will look at how customers can turn the Web from a threat into an opportunity for your company.

Key Tasks

Engaging Customer Advocates to Drive Your Marketing Strategy.

- Reframe traditional "push-pull" marketing by using an attraction approach through customer advocacy. Put customer content and stories at the forefront.

- To focus customer advocacy efforts, develop and maintain a marketing gravity chart and an accelerant curve that lets everyone in your organization know what you're doing to attract customers, and how you can accelerate the process most effectively.

- Establish thought leadership to escape dependence on external influencers and to exploit one of the most compelling branding opportunities in today's world for any firm: the IP you can create through your passionate customers combined with your best-in-class internal experts.

- Think expansively about how you can marshal customer advocates. They can help you get the word out about your firm and its offerings, penetrate new markets, and retain existing customers.

5

Harnessing the Internet

How Customers Can Turn the Web
from Threat into Opportunity for You

F IRMS THAT KNOW how to create an effective Web presence, one that attracts buyers and provides them with value when they're searching online, have a distinct advantage in today's market and into the future. As we've seen, it's the Internet and its myriad connections that customers will consult before they even think about buying from you.

Fortunately, as demonstrated in the last chapter, firms have precisely the resources they need to create powerful marketing gravity on the Web: internal subject-matter expertise, along with customers who have compelling stories to tell. Because, contrary to conventional wisdom, the Internet is not drowning in information. It's drowning in *bad* information. But it's starved for useful, credible content. Your customers and internal experts can fill that void while building your business and brand.

One division of a global enterprise software firm estimates that a full 70 percent of its "buyer's decision journey" takes place *before* a customer ever contacts a firm rep, and a great deal of that journey takes place on the Web. Increasingly, higher-level decision makers are searching the Web as well.[1] A 2009 Forbes Insights/Google study of 354 executives (director level or higher, at firms with revenues greater than $1 billion) found that the Internet is now the chief source of business information for such executives.[2] Of course, these are prospective buyers with large budgets who are hungry for solutions that will get them to where they want to go.

The Web and Its Discontents

That said, the Web presents a daunting challenge. With customers talking to each other and gathering information about you from third-party sources such as blogs, peer networks, and online communities, your reputation is at serious risk every day, as firms such as Dell, Maytag, Nestlé, Eurostar, and many others have discovered.[3] Even in the absence of such attacks, many corporate Web sites miss the boat on the substantial opportunities the Web presents, for three reasons.

First, it is extremely difficult for organizations to create a Web presence that is not "all about us"—to overcome a stubborn corporate narcissism that results in Web (and other media) communications that customers don't care about and often can't understand. Second is the difficulty all organizations have in understanding their customers and what they value. A third problem is that it can be difficult to keep up a fresh and relevant supply of peer information such as customer videos and testimonials—which is, among all the information you or others can provide customers and prospective buyers, the most highly valued.[4]

In this chapter we'll set out a Web strategy for overcoming these difficult issues and marshaling your customers and internal experts—and the highly sought-after information they can provide—into the mix. You'll learn how to protect your reputation, build marketing gravity, and generate leads; how to make use of technology to respond inexpensively to the "buyer's journey" with high volumes of persuasive customer content; and how to gain a clear vision of where the Web is headed and prepare for that.

But let's start with the basics: how to use the Web to build a brand like Intel did.

From "All About Us" to "More About You": How Intel Is Building Its Brand on the Web

Intel has been among the most diligent of firms when it comes to exploring and building expertise in its social media efforts.[5] That's because early on, Rhett Livengood, who runs the firm's global customer engagement programs, recognized opportunities to exploit the medium. For example, when Livengood learned that Intel's B2B social media team was engaging successfully with large audiences in its market—but lacked credible, regular content—he pulled out his trove of references from the firm's customers.

Still, Livengood acknowledges the skepticism surrounding the business value of social media programs. For one thing, many of these programs are pretty weak, with marketers posting traditional corporate messaging on social media sites. "But if you experiment intelligently," says Livengood, "and keep in mind the unique requirements of the medium (that is, don't try to control it) as well as its unique opportunities (that is, communities are starved for credible, relevant content) you absolutely can have significant impact on your business. And at a fraction of the cost of traditional marketing approaches."

Here are some lessons learned at Intel during its social media journey.

Bring Customer Advocates—and Buyers, Wherever They Are—into the Conversation

At first Livengood began posting the company's customer success stories on its Intel.com Web site. "These got some hits, but the number was not inspiring," says Livengood. "Perhaps a hundred or so per month for our most popular stories."

Over time he began to crack the code on how to exploit this new medium. He realized that his marketing efforts would go nowhere if confined to the corporate Web site. "We figured out where our customers and prospects were going, and went there ourselves," says Livengood. This included posting customer content on widely used public social networks such as Facebook, LinkedIn, and Twitter, along with other firms' Web sites with which its customers and potential buyers were engaging. "The idea of participating in conversations on other firms' sites was not an easy one to sell internally," says Livengood. "But eventually we realized we had to do it and in fact, that we wanted to do it. This new medium requires it."

The rewards have proven substantial: over a period of about eighteen months, for example, hits on Intel's customer success stories increased tenfold, playing a central role in turning Intel's Web social media program into a digital-age marketing and sales machine.

Exploit Your Unique Ability to Create Thought Leadership

Intel draws on several sources for content. It recruited technology and business experts from within the ranks to provide thought leadership, for example. "The mind-set had to be much different from the usual marketing pitch," says Livengood. "You can't have executives posting fluff. We learned pretty quickly that the community just won't stand for that. They want straight answers with candid, specific information, the good and the bad. When we learned to provide that, our credibility, and following, grew accordingly."

Intel also engaged with recognized experts in the field as well as members of the press and other media. And it engaged with new experts who emerged from within the ranks of the communities—including its own and other non-Intel communities.

Expand Your Notion of How Customers Can Participate

As Intel continued to add its customers into the conversation, Livengood and his team found new uses for them that fit the new medium. "No matter how hard we work to gain the trust of buyers, we're not 'one of them.' Our customers are. They can provide a customer's-eye view of how our solutions actually work. They can respond to inaccurate or even inflammatory comments online with facts from the horse's mouth. And perhaps most important, they can provide credible numbers showing business impact and ROI of the technology and solutions we and our partners provide."

Take Full Advantage of the Variety of Media Available

As Livengood and his team have learned to "repurpose" the firm's vault of customer reference content, the company's social media efforts have given new life to the superb source of information the Web provides. In addition to text that shows the issue addressed, solution provided, and resulting business impact, the digital versions can also provide video clips of customer testimonials, links to demos, and links to other information that the community has indicated interest in—providing superb illustrations of how the Web can enhance the staid customer story.

"Learning how to present information in a Web-friendly way is important of course," says Livengood. "But the real key to unleashing this content is to make sure that it addresses issues that the community is raising."

Develop Metrics That Measure Engagement and Movement Through the Buying Cycle

What has the integration of customer content and experts into Intel's social media programs produced? Significant business impact over the last three years. Among the gains that Intel can mention publicly: customer contacts generated by Intel's social media sites have increased from ten per month to hundreds per month, and page views of key customer content on Intel.com (which used to lie dormant) have exploded a hundredfold per month.

In addition, Livengood recognized a substantial opportunity to enhance Intel's brand and repute among IT decision makers, because of the increasingly larger B2B audience visiting its social media sites. To assess brand impact, Intel looks at how engaged its social media communities are—in particular, how often community members comment on Intel-authored blog posts and how often community members initiate discussions. Their goals are to achieve a one-to-nine-to-ninety ratio. That is, for every one hundred community members, one will comment regularly, nine will occasionally contribute content, and the other ninety will "lurk," or consume content without contributing to it.[6]

"We work hard to make sure our involvement in communities is—and appears to be—fair, transparent, and with equal control and influence compared to other voices," says Livengood. "And this applies just as much on our own Intel.com site."

Such transparency becomes crucial if the conversation in cyberspace begins to sour.

Take *Your* Reputation Out of *Their* Hands

No matter how nicely you play in the sand pile, the dark side of the Web is the damage a single disgruntled customer or angry activist can cause to your reputation. But companies are finding that attacks on the Web can provide an opportunity to demonstrate transparency and even convert angry customers into strong advocates. Preparedness is everything.

Be Sure You Have a Rapid Response Team in Place Before an Attack Arises

When journalism professor Jeff Jarvis blogged about his dismal experience after buying a Dell laptop (memorably calling it "Dell Hell"), Dell had no idea how to respond. As Jarvis suffered with the laptop that he couldn't get fixed despite his expensive four-year warranty, it created a media firestorm and PR nightmare that could have been easily avoided.[7] Other examples abound, such as the breakdown of five Eurostar trains that stranded thousands of passengers for hours on both sides of the English Channel, many in the tunnels, with no food, water, or communications from Eurostar officials about what was going on.

When such serious problems erupt, or a blogger or commentator decides to take you on, you can't wait two weeks to assemble a team, start preparing responses, and wait until legal approves them. You need to have communicators in place on all the social media and Web channels where your audience is found, and a process for mobilizing them quickly to deal with a serious attack on your reputation.

Have Content or Product Experts—
Not Marketing People—Respond

It's best to use people who are adept at listening to what customers are saying about you and responding attentively, rather than going directly into response mode with canned corporate messaging. And make sure that your company responds to criticism with facts. If you don't have them, say so, promise to get them, and then get them. Also, respond to anger with empathy. Not the canned empathy that many call center representatives read to you, but the real thing. As they say, anger and love are closely related: taking care of an angry customer in the right way can turn her into a passionate advocate. Respond to complaints with fixes. The team you have in place to respond to issues must have access and power to get them fixed quickly. Be sure to include senior executives in your rapid response team—and train them. Companies have floundered by using senior executive bloggers who don't understand the medium. Senior executives who talk plainly, recognize legitimate complaints, and get them fixed can add great value to your reputation management process.

Above All, Embrace the Opportunity
Presented by Transparency

True transparency can be painful, especially where it's needed the most—on issues where you have real problems that expose your vulnerability. But embracing it will enhance your reputation on the Web, where there's a low tolerance for corporate-speak or spin. It will also improve your organization.

When Salesforce.com struggled with Web site outages—a major problem for a company that delivers its CRM services through the Internet—customers started to complain about reliability. A competitor even signed up for the service and began to alert the press when the site was down. The outages revealed a significant problem: although uptime for its servers was still 99 percent, the code on which the SFDC platform was based wasn't scaling properly and required substantial rework. As savvy as he had been about customer and market relationships, CEO Marc Benioff then made a serious mistake: he decided to stop communicating to the market until the problem was fixed. As the outages got worse—at one point the service went down for ninety minutes—the firm's silence deepened the firm's perception problem as both bloggers and journalists demanded answers.

Some SFDC executives wanted to publish the firm's internal monitoring system so that customers could see the real-time status of its system, but even though transparency was an important value at the firm, Benioff hesitated: why allow competitors and the press to see embarrassing details every time the system slowed or went down? In the end, however, Benioff decided to "let go of his fears" and authorized creation of a trust.salesforce.com Web site that provided complete information on the firm's system performance, planned maintenance, system speed, and so forth. That restored trust with customers. It also provided great relief to SFDC executives. "Instead of hiding behind our problems, we started educating customers, prospects, and journalists on the issue," says Benioff. "It was liberating not to have to act defensively."

SFDC enjoyed an additional benefit from "going public." Doing so improved the performance of the organization, by adding a new and very visible level of accountability.

Increase Your Marketing Gravity on the Web by Responding to the Buyer's Decision Journey

Effective company Web sites can accelerate the development of customer relationships by providing content that attracts prospective buyers based on where they are in the buying process. Figure 5-1 provides an overview of how to do so, based on the fact that peer information is the first or second most trusted source of information *at each stage* of the buyer's decision journey—from awareness and education to finding a solution to, finally, selecting what to purchase.

Breaking into the Buyer's Comfort Zone: The Awareness and Education Phase

In terms of marketing gravity, this is the most "remote" phase, where a potential buyer may not know you exist and is likely not

FIGURE 5-1

The buyer's decision journey

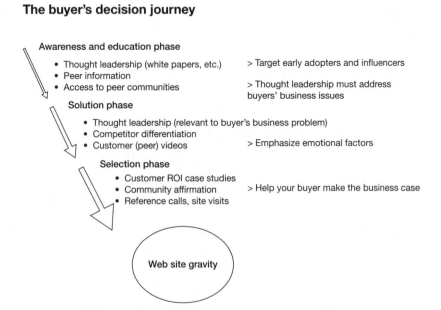

even aware that he needs what you can provide. For example, such a prospect could be an executive of a manufacturing firm that suffers from inefficiencies in its computer systems without realizing it or knowing that it is giving an edge to more technologically advanced competitors.

The challenge is to move the potential customer away from comfort with the status quo, to make the buyer aware that he has a problem or opportunity that can be addressed and that he has peers—in particular, your customers—who are doing so successfully. Your best shot here is with buyers and influencers who keep abreast of current trends, new technologies, new manufacturing approaches, and the like. Effective sources of information include talking to peers in communities or live events.

Intel, as we've seen, participates diligently in such conversations and puts customer stories front and center where applicable to the conversation. In addition, good companies will have internal experts such as Hu Yoshida, the CTO at Hitachi Data Systems who provides first-rate insights into the industry trends that buyers in the awareness stage are looking for, with blog posts such as "Top 10 [Industry] Trends for 2011." Influencers in your audience who encounter such information are likely to pass it along to other prospective buyers in their networks. When such Web efforts are combined with live events such as Salesforce.com's City Tours or HDS's major city seminars, the result is powerful awareness building—as well as relationship building—with prospective buyers.

Breaking Through the Noise: The Solution or "Considering a Change" Phase

At this phase the buyer understands the general nature of her problem, is open to a change, and is ready to start considering solutions. Your Web efforts therefore need to attract her with value, and help move her from exploring possible solutions to getting her to seriously consider and commit to yours.

Emotional factors are important. They will likely include reluctance to make a change that will add to her already burdensome work load, as well as the risk that implementing a change will backfire or unleash unintended consequences that will create more problems down the road.

Because they are ready to explore possible solutions, buyers at this stage are particularly open to content from vendors *provided* it has exceptional value, including content that

- Addresses emotional factors at play

- Demonstrates command of issues the buyer is dealing with, *in her terms*

- Establishes expertise and thought leadership on the specific *business* problem the buyer is dealing with that you can help solve

- Includes relevant information or access to such information from the buyer's peers, including your customers

At this stage, customer testimonials—from people who have things in common with the prospective buyer—can be very powerful. These don't need to be expensive, high-production-value affairs. For example, in one customer video, John Damiano, an Atlanta real estate broker, describes how a small Web design firm called Bella Web Design helped him make sense of social media.[8] He also describes how the firm is helping to build his business. Even more compelling, a viewer experiences Damiano's emotional response: his sense of pride that he's now perceived as being on top of this new media and at the forefront of his industry, as well as his excitement at how the firm has helped him establish new relationships and, together with live events, build his community of customers.

Providing the Ammo: The Selection Phase

At this stage, buyers have committed to your solution and need to move toward justifying the selection and persuading other customer stakeholders to make the decision. Affirmation from traditional sources, such as relevant third parties like customer references and industry analysts, is particularly important here. An especially powerful tool, for example, is ROI customer case studies showing what business impact your customers have achieved with your solution.

Position Your Web Strategy for the Future

It may seem like folly to predict how corporate digital strategies will evolve over the next few years, but in fact some aspects of that evolution are predictable: it will still be human beings with whom these organizations are interacting. Many of the major changes in knowledge creation and dissemination created by the Web are already well established. So, what's coming?

- *Company advocates and experts will emerge as thought leaders on the Web.* This is especially important in the early and middle stages of the buyer's decision journey. Marketing copy posted prominently on corporate Web sites or Facebook pages will increasingly give way to conversations with buyer peers and thought leaders, along with the content that buyers find through search engines and peer recommendations. Company bloggers will include executives who address their buyers' agendas knowledgeably. Company Web sites and communities will feature customer advocates who speak the buyer's language. Companies must know how prospective buyers are using the Web to keep abreast of industry trends.

  For example, what are the terms your buyers are searching on Google? A valuable exercise: search some possible terms and see what turns up from your firm. Companies will ask, Does our expert who's blogging on the issue come up high on search engine rankings? Are buyers finding our customer videos that address the buyer's issues?

- *Company Web sites will provide more value to customers, and more acceleration to higher value.* Company Web site teams will become increasingly adept at providing immediate value to the visiting prospect—and the technology is there for organizations to understand what the buyer needs and where he is in the buying cycle, to provide the knowledge and information he needs, and to harvest rich information *about* the buyer in order to improve his experience. If the prospect is in the pre-awareness phase, he will quickly get to thought leadership pieces alerting him to new issues and approaches in his industry. If she's in the "considering alternatives" phase, she'll get to videos of customers describing how they made their decision. This applies to the existing customer as well, and even the satisfied customer—there will be new value targeted to her as well when she returns to your Web site.

- *Company Web sites will provide easy access to peer information and peer interaction.* That's an obvious feature of the Web site of the future, since peer information is most valued by prospective buyers and customers—a reality to which even luxury retail brands are bowing. Firms will provide access to peer communities, sometimes formed by the company itself, sometimes not. Buyers want to know what their peers think of your products and solutions. Why not make it easy for them to find out? In addition, company Web sites will increasingly provide buyers with access to customers using technology that matches them in ways in which both buyer and customer reference are agreeable. The customer information that companies provide will also increasingly graduate from individual customer information to statistics and trends showing the experience of customers across entire industries (see the section "Automate Customer Content Creation" later in this chapter).

- *Company Web sites will be organized and even developed to reflect how knowledge is created and disseminated on the Web.* Although the many "revolutions" supposedly being spawned by the Web are often hype (e.g., that social media tools are spawning actual political revolutions), there is one that is quite real: the way in which knowledge is being created and organized. For example, the hierarchical model of knowledge creation, in which credentialed, titled, or certified experts are in charge of what's "fit to print"—which is at best a seriously imperfect system—will increasingly give way to knowledge created by the community. That approach, once thought fanciful and anarchic (particularly by those same traditional "experts"), is clearly taking hold on the Web.[9]

What's more, the most effective corporate Web sites will embrace this because (1) that's the way knowledge is being developed on the Web and (2) it is known that the approach can be at least as effective as the traditional one.[10] Effective corporate Web sites will, as much as possible, make available or provide access to *all* knowledge relevant to the buyer or prospect and provide ways for him to comment or otherwise participate in the conversation.

Make Good Use of Video

The use of video is in its infancy: corporate Web sites will increasingly make better use of it. For instance, in 2011 Salesforce. com announced that it was diverting 69 percent of its traditional demand-generation budgets to customer videos and social media. This reflects not just advances in technology, but an ancient human trait. We're used to learning by seeing. Learning by reading text is a relatively recent invention with limited effectiveness.

As TED's Chris Anderson has shown, using video himself, the Internet and increasingly inexpensive video devices are making it possible for break dancers and extreme sports athletes to easily exchange videos that create far-flung rapid-learning communities who can *see* how to make the next leading-edge move. The result is rapid development of the state of the art that would have previously been impossible. The Internet and inexpensive video technology is also allowing poor villagers in Africa to collaborate and exchange techniques to improve farming productivity in their villages, resulting in remarkable innovations. It's also allowing scientists to improve the speed of their research efforts, because colleagues who want to test the accuracy of the results can *show* each other much more precisely how the experiment was performed than they can ever *tell* through traditional text.

Organizational Web sites will similarly become much more adept at showing customers and prospects how to address—and particularly, how their *peers* are addressing—the issues they're interested in. Some of video's benefits include the following:

- *Video will do more to convey the customer's emotion.* This isn't just about showing that the customer is happy or pleased. It means letting her tell her story. It means thinking through the question, What was the underlying emotional driver that caused her to buy—and that presumably our firm has delivered on? Every experienced salesperson knows that it was an emotional driver that caused the customer to buy. It might be a sense of reduced stress because your solution enables so much more productivity than the one she had before. Or a sense of security because yours is more dependable. High production values, music, and other devices don't convey this nearly as well as the customer herself, unscripted, talking in the moment about this with real feeling.

- *Video will show what your solution did.* So many videos have the customers just telling what happened—hardly the best use of a medium that's so adept at showing! It may seem difficult to show what a complex technological solution does in a way that can be quickly grasped by a prospect who knows very little about it, but leading-edge firms will start cracking that code. Management consultants have grown extremely skilled at creating process visuals—illustrated charts, diagrams, and so forth—that convey the gist of complex concepts in ways that mere text descriptions can never match. Video should be able to adapt that approach and take it up a notch.

- *Customer videos will facilitate idea sharing.* Why not encourage your customer communities to share ideas using video, perhaps using a modified YouTube-type section on your community site? Among the many benefits of this, in addition to ideas for your product development people, is that you would likely get additional footage that would make terrific testimonials. If poor villagers in Africa can collaborate remotely to improve farming techniques, why can't your customers collaborate to expand how they're using your product?

- *Customer videos will help qualify the buyer.* Some customer videos could do more to qualify the buyer and make sure he gets to the videos and other information on your Web site that are most relevant to his situation. Instead of relying on a system of Web site categories and links that require the customer to navigate his way to the right video, why not provide an elegant and entertaining video that does the work for him? For example, marketing automation firm Eloqua developed a Groundswell Award–winning interactive video called "The Conversation" that engages prospects in an entertaining dialogue to determine what their needs are, then directs them quickly to resources that can provide immediate help.

- *Customer videos will do more to interact with the buyer.* Marketing departments will regard the video as one part of the engagement process, which accelerates the buyer to deeper and more intimate engagement with the firm. After getting the buyer emotionally involved, providing compelling information and substantial value, he'll want more. Videos can interact with him to determine where he would like to go next: to a teleconference, demo, event, online community, or so forth.

Automate Customer Content Creation: The Future Is Now

We've seen that customer content is the gold standard for marketing and sales enablement communications. Creating such content for many firms is mired in old and increasingly cumbersome processes. Technology, the Web, and entrepreneurial innovation are making it possible to overcome these barriers, which is no surprise, given the substantial economic rewards for doing so.

Creating customer case studies or success stories, for example, is often a frustrating and much too expensive process. Many customers—particularly those from "big brand" high-visibility firms—are extremely wary of allowing their executives to be interviewed for such stories. If they do agree, the review process can be so time consuming and the editing of content so cautious that the final result is old and toothless by the time it's published. Plus, the expense of hiring good writers who can track down and extract worthwhile information about significant business and emotional benefits from interviewees and produce a useful case study can be jaw-droppingly high—particularly in industries where a fresh supply of customer content is needed regularly.

Add to such constraints long-entrenched practices surrounding case studies (or "success stories")—that they emphasize only the "good news," leave out uncomfortable details about problems encountered during the relationship, and so on—and you can wind up with an overpriced story that buyers don't believe even when they take the time to read it.

It would seem that there's got to be a better way. And there is.

Creating Compelling Customer Content Rapidly and Inexpensively

Companies such as Dell, EMC, Hewlett-Packard, and Hitachi Data Systems are capitalizing on new technologies to create compelling customer content. Using a sophisticated yet simple e-mail survey process, such firms poll customers periodically during the year about how they're extracting value from the firms' solutions. The surveys are easily taken in a few minutes, with perhaps eight to ten questions, including a comments box in which happy customers put testimonials. The survey is conducted and results are analyzed not by the firm, but by a verified third-party validation service.

Further, the analysis is generated *immediately,* as survey responses start coming in.

Using this process, data storage and information management firm Hitachi Data Systems can tell its market (through a company blogger) that, for example:

> *86% of the organizations surveyed {who use an HDS system} increased their performance by 10 to 25% or more compared to other enterprise storage systems in their prior environment. In a majority of cases (over 50%) performance was the reason for purchasing the platform (source: TechValidate). According to the survey, customers who purchased USPs found reduced operational costs between 10 and 25% of their storage administration costs compared to prior environments.*
>
> *Focusing on our File and Content Services portfolio, the survey also identified that 35% of IT organizations increased their application performance between 20 to 30% after deploying their Hitachi High-performance NAS platform; 52% of IT organizations increased the application performance between 10 and 20 percent after deployment (source: TechValidate).* [11]

Note that the information offered is not only compelling to potential buyers but also has considerable interest to other HDS *customers* who want to know if they're getting the value from the firm's solutions that their peers are.

In addition, firms using this approach can auto-generate *marketing content* immediately. As the survey is being taken, the firm can see aggregated data and individual customer testimonials as they come in. Once finished, the software can auto-generate industry reports using aggregated data, as well as short individual case studies showing the problem solved, solution used, and business benefits achieved. These can be pasted into marketing communication pieces such as press releases and on Web and social media sites. They can also be stored on auto-generated company Web pages by industry, solution, and other categories useful to sales and marketing for easy access. The platform can also create portal Web pages to keep a running total of how a particular *industry* is benefiting from its solutions.

———————

Leading companies have moved beyond fearing the threat that the Web can represent—the dangers *are* manageable—and have begun to focus on the opportunities it provides.

Most important, buyers are looking for ideas and solutions on the Web. You can provide them. Far from losing control over the conversation, you can in fact exert substantial influence through the twin assets of passionate customers and internal experts, communicating in many ways to targeted audiences without the barriers of traditional media.

All of which leads nicely into the next chapter, where I'll show you how your customers can help you build a veritable community around your products or services.

Key Tasks

Engaging Customer Advocates to Increase Your Web Presence.

- Buyers—even executive business buyers—are increasingly looking for solutions on the Web. Engage them there by providing real value, not "marketingese."

- Focus your Web strategy on where your buyers are. That said, you *can* increase the gravity of your corporate Web site by learning where buyers are in their decision journey and responding to it.

- The most powerful content comes from your customers, together with internal experts addressing buyers' issues.

- Don't market on the Web; engage buyers in conversation in order to establish a relationship and build trust—two of the most important steps in the buying process.

- Protect your reputation with transparency and responsiveness. If you can achieve this, it will have a salutary effect on your organization and its performance.

- Position your Web site for a fast-approaching future in which peer content and video will be kings.

6

Building Customer Communities in a Networked World

How Customers and Companies Are Doing Together What They Can't Do Alone

MORE THAN THIRTY YEARS AGO, McKinsey consultants Tom Peters and Bob Waterman began urging companies to "get close to customers" as part of a firm project to identify and spread best corporate organizational practices among its clients. It later became a separate chapter title in their blockbuster book *In Search of Excellence.*[1] But how many companies have actually achieved that ideal? Although firms sink buckets full of cash into understanding customers better, improving relationships with them, and, more recently, turning them into "promoters," their goal of doing so simply to get customers to buy more stuff has been, as we've seen, shortsighted to say the least.

You can begin to unlock the value of your customer relationships by nurturing your advocates, influencers, and contributors toward building customer communities. Such communities can help build brand, create marketing gravity, generate leads, improve strategy and innovation, and substantially offset the loss of control of the conversation created by the Internet and social media. As SAP's Salim Ali, global vice president of enterprise solutions and community marketing, notes, he would rather market directly to SAP's various communities—numbering more than two million customers, prospects, and partners—than through a purchased database.

Why does community marketing work so well? Because there's a good chance your customers will want to associate with each other and you, as we'll see. More firms can build thriving customer communities than think they can. But many firms stumble badly when trying to do so—the Web landscape is littered with ambitious social media programs that quickly and ignominiously bit the dust.

A common mistake is to start with a "social media strategy." The Internet is a superb tool for building far-flung networks, connecting people around the world, and allowing them to share a broad array of information freely or almost freely. Yet the notion that social media can form people into cohesive associations that can get meaningful things done is badly misguided. Whatever a customer community is, it's not Facebook.

I see a lot of people confusing or interchanging "communities" with networks, tribes, ecosystems, and other social groups. The notion of forming customers into "tribes" is particularly popular now, and especially misguided. Tribes—if we're using the term according to its historical meaning—are exclusionary. Membership is based on arbitrary criteria such as race, kinship, or ethnicity. They're also hierarchical, autocratic, enamored of tradition, and suspicious of outsiders.

Communities, on the other hand, tend to be inclusive meritocracies formed around a common set of values. It doesn't matter what your color, race, or heritage is. What matters is whether you share the community's interests and values. The most dynamic communities embrace member empowerment over hierarchy, value education over tradition, and welcome diversity as a source of creativity. Rather than shun outsiders, communities ask, "How can we grow something greater than any of us could do alone?" Communities form the fundamental social building blocks of America, the most natural way in which we develop associations with others.[2]

As we'll see, we're on the verge of a tremendous boom in community building today, fueled in part by the Internet. As it happens, Americans are quite good at building communities. After all, we've been doing it for four hundred years.

This chapter will help you ride this coming trend and offers a framework for community marketing, while helping you avoid the sorts of failures we see when companies try to build their own customer communities. First let's start with some context, and then illustrate why communities are natural building blocks for corporations.

What Every Executive Should Know About Communities

Communities didn't appear with the introduction of Internet chat rooms. They've been around a long time, particularly in America, and we have a lot of history to guide us in the dynamics of successful community building and how to tap the considerable economic power communities can generate for a firm.

Americans Are Superb at Community Building

During his now-celebrated visit to America in 1831, the French intellectual Alexis de Tocqueville was astonished at a phenomenon the world had not seen before—the rapid development of thriving towns, cities, voluntary associations, and ultimately an entire civilization, without any sort of hierarchical authority in charge and directing things. In fact, concluded de Tocqueville, no hierarchical authority could have done so.[3]

In New England, for example, despite the persistent difficulties presented by harsh weather and infertile soil, New Englanders built the most entrepreneurial communities in America and, indeed, the world. When they found they couldn't farm, they quickly adapted and became expert and wealthy fishermen. Then they transformed again into sea traders and merchants. In the early eighteenth century during an embargo that cut off America's shipping trade, the New Englanders transformed themselves again into factory builders, spearheading the Industrial Revolution in America. The concepts of "Yankee ingenuity" and "the Protestant work ethic" grew out of the New England community builders, starting with the Massachusetts Bay Company in 1630.

That same cohesion and economic vibrancy repeated itself again and again as immigrant Americans from around the world perfected this community-building model. For example, Benjamin Franklin's Junto helped build members' careers along with significant parts of Philadelphia; the Ohio Associates and the Green and Jersey Company helped settle the American West; twentieth-century associations such as Rotary and Kiwanis clubs combined community service with professional camaraderie; and now twenty-first-century software user and apps groups help solve one another's problems. All of these groups faced the same issue: the need to *associate* to solve problems, make sense of a complex world, and pursue opportunities—without waiting for some authority to move in and do it for them.

No one attempting to build a community—if they're serious about it—should be without an understanding of this remarkable four-hundred-year-old social dynamic. Especially now, since we may be on the threshold of a new worldwide explosion in forming and developing communities.

The Coming Boom in Community Building

At the turn of the twentieth century, the United States experienced an astonishing revolution in community building and inventiveness. Over a period of just fifty years, from 1870 to 1920, an explosion in community building established most of the foundations for civic life for the twentieth century, with the continental expansion of established associations such as the Masons and the creation of dozens of major new associations such as the Rotary club, the Red Cross, the Boy Scouts, the American Bar Association, Goodwill, the American Nurses Association, the United Way (originally, the Community Chest), and dozens of others. Many of these associations grew rapidly to memberships of hundreds of thousands, with chapters around the country.

The major reason? Associations were better able than individuals to address scores of the new challenges and opportunities facing Americans and the immigrants who came here—and the mind-boggling complexity that accompanied them.[4] Like the early twenty-first century, world-changing new technologies proliferated—such as railroads, the telegraph, electricity, the telephone, and automobiles, along with new forms of enterprise and production—making far-reaching new connections between people possible on a scale never before known and bringing waves of people from farms to shops and factories in increasingly crowded cities.

Along with the fabulous opportunities that a newly connected world was opening up came a sense of confusion and dislocation that we can hardly imagine, as historian Robert Putnam describes:

> {A}n immigrant raised as a peasant in a Polish village little changed from the sixteenth century . . . within a few years was helping to construct the avant-garde skyscrapers of Louis Sullivan in the city of "big shoulders" beside Lake Michigan.[5]

Entrepreneurs and business leaders were hardly less perplexed, as they had to develop new forms of business, organization, and production to exploit the opportunities before them while avoiding the equally formidable pitfalls. Americans formed so many work, professional, and civic associations because no person alone confronting such an overwhelmingly complex world could hope to succeed by relying on slow-to-respond institutions already in place.

As Putnam points out, our own world is strikingly similar. Businesses today, including your own and those of your customers, are likewise dealing with daunting complexity in a world that is again grappling with new technologies that are connecting us in ways we'd never imagined: increasingly interconnected economies, enterprises, societies, and governments. Although these create vast new opportunities, such unprecedented interconnectedness also creates interdependencies that are poorly understood, making the consequences of any decision hard to anticipate. Volatility, exacerbated by unfamiliar new markets, uncertain political factors, and increasing regulation, is now the new normal, adding additional layers of complexity to the mix.

As in turn-of-the-century America, this environment is creating a new need for association that our experience with community building can answer. Fortunately, successful corporations have long found themselves drawing on community-building principles— such as cooperating for a greater good, establishing mutually agreed-upon values, and strong ethical standards—in order to bond people and energize them toward meeting common goals.[6] For example, Microsoft, as I'll discuss in chapter 7, has had great success in forming a remarkable, high-level council of marquee-name CIOs from around the world into its Interoperability Executive Customer (IEC) Council because of the urgent need for cooperation in order to get its increasingly diverse and complex technology platforms to work together properly.

Likewise, David Packard and Bill Hewlett developed the HP Way, a set of deeply considered values that guided the firm for decades and helped it avoid rash decisions and ethical mine fields. Even crusty Jack Welch, not particularly known as the touchy-feely sort, spent years developing and clarifying General Electric's values, as we'll see, as part of his effort to rebuild the culture of a stagnant firm. He also introduced the New England town-hall approach to company meetings through his famous Work Out concept.

Companies that can help their customers meet their rapidly growing needs for new associations and community may be on the cusp of a dramatic new opportunity. Let's look now at how to get started.

How to Build Vibrant Customer Communities

Rather than ask, "What is our social media strategy?" organizations should ask, "What sort of group of people are we forming? What will attract them? How will they interact? What purpose will it serve? What business impact will it have for our organization?"

CSC, for example, which develops software that helps financial services firms run their businesses, has a particularly successful online community called WikonnecT and has used social media—such as blogs, message boards, chat sessions, and the like—to enhance it. The strength of WikonnecT, however, doesn't come from the social media tools that enhance the online experience. It comes from the fact that CSC is creating communities.

The firm's community-building efforts began, like many software firms, with a user group of coders. For years they've gathered in live meetings at least once a year, along with an elected board of clients that helps CSC prioritize spending on specific development projects.

In addition, the firm has built higher-level advisory councils that attract customer executives with larger budgets to discuss issues such as policy issuance, claims processing, and billing and collections, providing valuable input into CSC's strategic direction. CSC has also built midlevel operational boards and working groups that help the firm streamline its software, make sure it does what it's supposed to do, and avoid development rework. Another community focuses on innovation, with member clients submitting requests for system changes and improvements.

That foundation—of a community committed to mutual goals—was the basis for the subsequent success of the social media component, WikonnecT. So when it comes to building customer communities, or even just understanding how they work so you can engage with them, there's no need to reinvent the wheel. We have several centuries of experience on which to draw.

Social Media Strategy Is an Oxymoron

Social media is a collection of tools—and there are many others—that can enhance community building (figure 6-1).

FIGURE 6-1

Social media: one of many communication and community building tools

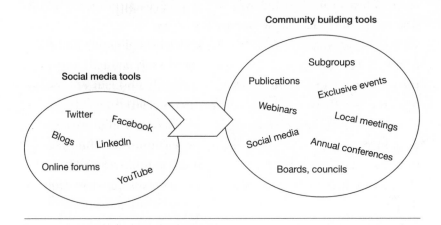

Community building tools

Social media tools

Twitter   Facebook
Blogs   LinkedIn
Online forums   YouTube

Subgroups
Publications   Exclusive events
Webinars   Local meetings
Social media   Annual conferences
Boards, councils

Communities: Helping Customers Achieve High-Value Goals

Time and again during the settlement of America, people would bond together in community to achieve what they couldn't do alone. They had to in order to build settlements, organize an economy, build roads and bridges, provide for a common defense, and pursue economic opportunities. No monarch, guild, or other hierarchical authority could reach them or otherwise manage such tasks.

Today we see this spirit all the time as customers form their own communities—for example, to provide each other the service they can't get from their vendors. But forming communities can fry much bigger fish than that. Hewlett-Packard's healthcare and public-sector businesses, for example, are forming an industrywide community to help 800,000 US physicians, perhaps half of whom need to seriously upgrade their IT systems to keep up with the complex requirements of electronic healthcare record keeping. No one company could possibly meet this need, and even if it could, most physicians prefer to work with local vendors. Therefore HP is forming a community of local healthcare providers and vendors around the United States to work together to tackle this opportunity in a comprehensive way that neither the providers nor HP could achieve alone.

Companies that seek to form customer communities need to be aware of their awkward position: if they attempt to play a dominant role, they'll destroy an important dynamic. HP, for example, must take care not to play or be seen to play an authoritarian role.

Now for the nitty-gritty. The rest of this section describes specific ways that you can build a community that will attract and serve your customers (see figure 6-2.)

Organize Around a Shared Purpose

What makes communities different from, and more powerful than, networks or tribes is the common purpose: it's about the *members,* not about sacred traditions or the imperatives of organizers. (Be sure to remind your marketing department!) SFDC customer communities especially embrace that value, helping customer-members learn from each other how to succeed in their jobs, find new jobs when needed, and pursue personal and professional growth and more.

Similarly, Benjamin Franklin's Junto, which started as a small group of young nobodies in Philadelphia, went on to make major contributions to the city. It helped to establish superb institutions such as a volunteer fire department, a militia, a city library (the first subscription library in America), the Philadelphia Academy (now the University of Pennsylvania), and the Pennsylvania Hospital. The Junto was not the creature of city leaders, but was formed by Franklin and others to advance their own small businesses while looking for opportunities to help the larger community.

This doesn't mean that customer communities should or need be an exercise in altruism for companies. Massachusetts, for example, was settled by the Massachusetts Bay *Company.* The key is creating exceptional *mutual* value.

FIGURE 6-2

Community gravity

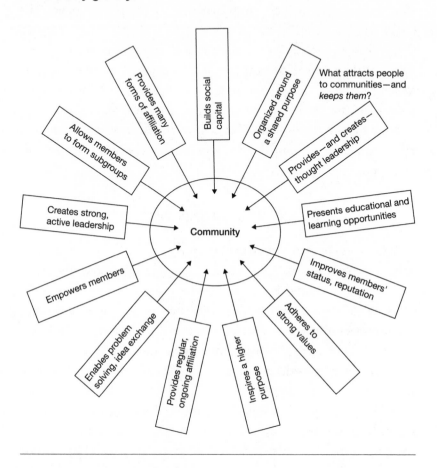

CSC's WikonnecT platform, for example, is designed for members to follow the progress of product releases they're interested in. It allows them to sign up for RSS feeds to receive updates, and enables them to provide input in the form of comments and ratings. "When companies set up collaboration communities for their clients, they tend to start pushing marketing information—this is what our product does, and you really need to buy it," says Dawn Cochran, CIO of the firm's property and casualty business, who oversees WikonnecT. "We say this is what our product does, these are some of the issues we have; let's collaborate to make it better so you'll get a better result." That approach works because of the reputation CSC has built in its communities over the years—as a firm that wants its customers to succeed.

What follows are important professional and personal needs that your community should work to satisfy. The first three needs (provide many forms of regular, ongoing affiliation and relationship building; improve reputation and status; and offer access to thought leadership) are the most critical. The last three needs are very nice to have for more ambitious communities. Getting the right mix for your particular community can create powerful attraction.

Provide Many Forms of Regular, Ongoing Affiliation and Relationship Building

Peer relationships are among the most highly valued things people can have. In a business context, they provide an opportunity to learn from each other, exchange ideas, network for jobs, and, perhaps most important, affiliate with people who understand each other. Simple affiliation with kindred spirits is a powerful emotional bond. You can't really understand how powerful this is for a community until you experience it first hand. In my own communities of marketing and customer engagement professionals—the people who implement many of the programs described in this book—I see this constantly at live events. It's fantastic when someone I've just met comes up to me with a broad smile and says, "I can't tell you how wonderful it is to be around people who understand what I go through every day!"

Improve Reputation and Status

In professional communities especially, members will spend significant time building their reputations. It's worthwhile building a good reputation system that allows community members to recognize worthy individual contributions, as well as contributors who provide such contributions over a period of time, such as Jeff

Stenski, who's recognized as a "Diamond contributor" on the Dell customer forum for the tens of thousands of posts he's made.

Offer Access to Thought Leadership

Providing thought leadership—a sense that *this* is a source of information that one can't be without—creates powerful community gravity. As mentioned, companies are in an excellent position to provide this with the one-two punch of peer (customer) stories plus in-house content experts.

That said, communities are about *educating* their members, and that means providing access to the *best* information in the world, not just *your* information. Why not also provide access to worthy information from *any* source, as long as it meets the needs of members? Of course if you find that you're relying on outside information too much, you may need to take another look at how well you're tapping your own internal resources. You don't want to go from being thought leader to information aggregator.

For more ambitious communities, the following three needs also will be important to satisfy for your members.

Build Social Capital

Some communities will see building social capital as a mandate as well. A concept developed by Robert Putnam, Ronald Burt, and others, social capital has an important application to customer and other business communities.[7] Succeeding economically in complex environments requires a dynamic network of relationships that in itself provides high value. Wells Fargo executive vice president Steve Ellis captures the concept when he describes the value of the bank's industry advisory councils, consisting of senior executives from a variety of firms within key industries for the bank, such as energy or transportation: "You learn how the council members work together. You learn about the industry. You make new connections and then you help them make new connections."

Venture capitalist Eric Litman abandoned the world of venture capital to start a business in response to what he perceived as a major opportunity, provided he could get to market quickly. He formed a business called Medialets to provide an ad network for mobile applications, or apps. Within days of sketching out a strategy, Litman had a high-quality team of fourteen people in place to launch the firm. Barely a month after that the company had a product to take to market. He was able to move so quickly because of the extensive and relevant network of relationships he'd built up over the years.

An important question for community builders today is how to increase the creation of social capital among members. Doing so will not only increase the value of the community to them, but will also increase their value to the community.

Empower Members with Strong Community Leaders

Empowered is a much used and abused term, but in successful communities you'll see the real thing. Governance of great communities is based on mutual agreement among members who have a say in leadership selection. It creates messy situations at times—but those messy situations, if handled correctly, bind people further to the community.

As Dawn Cochran and her team built the online and social media extension of the company's communities, WikonnecT, they continually pulled customers into the process rather than trying to get it perfect before rolling it out. The process took several iterations, but in the end customers had a platform they were enthusiastic about. At its live customer events, CSC holds forums for customers to discuss future software development plans and seek customer input. The discussions are inevitably enlightening to CSC. Customers can then vote on the features they'd most like to see, and the top three choices go into the next release.

At its most vibrant, the concept of empowerment doesn't mean that lead organizers "confer" power on members, which implies that it can be withdrawn at will. Many of the most successful American communities were, in fact, self-formed. Their members couldn't wait for—or couldn't be reached—by some authority figure taking charge. In their earliest days, American settlements were literally in a wilderness that no authority could reach. They were built on a foundation of combining individual responsibility along with a say in governance. Advancement and leadership in vibrant American communities were based on a meritocracy.

The results were an impressive economic dynamism. In early Massachusetts, the Bay Company settlers cleared away Old World restraints such as guilds, permanent monopolies, and wage and price controls common in Europe and replaced them with innovations such as protection of private property, building market economies fueled by private venture capital, and above all reliance on the initiative and entrepreneurism of individuals.

Inspire a Higher Purpose

As the small group of Massachusetts Bay Company shareholders sailed to America in 1630 to start a new life, their leader John Winthrop said, "We shall be as a city on a hill, the eyes of all people are upon us." It was, and remains, perhaps the most inspiring vision for community ever articulated. Ronald Reagan would repeat those words nearly four hundred years later to revive the nation's economic dynamism and sense of purpose after a losing war in Vietnam, political scandal in Washington, a stagnant economy, and a general feeling of malaise in the country.

The Massachusetts Bay settlers came to America to seek economic opportunity, of course. But it was not their sole driving force. They placed equal importance on the opportunity to pursue their religious and moral ideals: to strive to live them every day rather than just talk about them on Sunday and, in so doing, to provide an example that others in the world could take inspiration from. Rather than hampering their economic success, that higher purpose fueled it. (The sidebar "National Instruments: A Rapid Jump Start in Building Customers for the Future" offers a good modern-day case in point.) The settlers' remarkable economic dynamism was the result of them pursuing both "material wealth and moral satisfaction," as the perceptive Tocqueville put it. "These two tendencies, apparently so discrepant, are far from conflicting: they advance together and support each other." A profound insight that many firms still miss.

Unify People Around Strong Values

Community values are not just platitudes that get posted on a Web site. They serve the critical purpose of binding community members who may have little else in common culturally and of establishing behaviors that will keep people pointed to community goals. In describing the remarkable explosion in membership of successful fraternal associations in the United States at the turn of the twentieth century, historian David T. Beito writes:

> By joining a lodge, an initiate adopted a set of values. Societies dedicated themselves to the advancement of mutualism, self-reliance, business training, thrift, leadership skills, self-government, and good moral character. These values reflected a fraternal consensus that cut across such seemingly intractable divisions as race, gender, and income.[8]

Which values? *Imposing* specific values on a community isn't a good idea. However, leaders can be guided by the fact that historically, successful communities have some form of the following three: reciprocity, trustworthiness, and civility. Their power comes not from stating them or putting them on a wall, but from actually practicing and enforcing them.

Legendary General Electric (GE) chairman Jack Welch took that approach when he tackled the herculean task of reforming GE's culture after a defense contract scandal had sullied the company's reputation, and the existence of deeply entrenched bureaucracies was stifling performance and innovation in the ninety-year-old firm. To do so, he wound up adopting many of the key traits that have made American communities so dynamic, which included taking the time and effort to develop a new values statement for the firm.

National Instruments: A Rapid Jump Start in Building Customers for the Future

In 2009, National Instruments (NI) faced a daunting challenge in marketing its robotics software platform, LabVIEW. Relatively new and unknown in its industry, NI had only a small fraction of market share relative to its main competitor. Getting people to convert—or, for that matter, getting industry media to take notice—would be difficult.

The key for NI was building a community that embraced a particularly inspiring larger purpose. The company had three things going for it. First, the LabVIEW platform was quite good. Second, although small in number, its customers were quite passionate—especially those using LabVIEW on the Macintosh and those who were using it to run LEGO's widely popular model building product, Mindstorms NXT. In addition, NI had long experience running large user communities among its broad user base of engineers and scientists in some thirty thousand companies around the world.

NI saw its opportunity to build community and substantially raise LabVIEW's profile through a popular robotics competition in Atlanta, called FIRST (For Inspiration and Recognition of Science and Technology). Dean Kamen, the philanthropist and inventor who runs the event, has a personal passion for getting young people interested in science and technology, a critical educational need for the United States. His FIRST competition attracts about 1,700 high school teams throughout the country and culminates in a Super Bowl–like event in the Georgia Dome each spring.

That event is what NI's vice president of product marketing, Ray Almgren, and his team focused on—building a community around FIRST. Their goal? To get these highly visible FIRST competitors—and potential customers of the future—to adopt the LabVIEW program in building their robots rather than the much more widely known competitor. But in addition to the firm's self-interest, a higher purpose was pursued with great passion: NI recruited existing NI LabVIEW customers to train and mentor these students.

Customers who participated received a series of increasingly sophisticated training modules that included online training, workshops, and even VIP events. NI built a lively ni.com/first Web site that included videos of "this week's featured team" running their robots, technical information to help teams solve problems, and community news. It also featured, of course, opportunities for students to collaborate with mentors and NI employees and partner firms who could provide specialized expertise while getting to know their peers who were also adopting LabVIEW.

"A key technology in helping us pull off the FIRST effort was our investment in our Web community platforms on ni.com," says John Pasquarette, vice president of e-business for NI. "We'd built out a flexible platform on our Web site enabling private groups, discussion forums, and knowledge bases that we've used for years to connect our customers in industry for user-driven technical support and solution sharing. That allowed us to quickly and inexpensively tap into our active user community to help make this happen."

NI also connected LabVIEW members based on geography to encourage in-person meetings and collaboration where possible and thus strengthen the new community. The firm also created recognition and awards programs not only for outstanding use of the platform but also to recognize valuable participation and support for the community itself.

The LabVIEW community launch was high risk for a relatively unknown platform. The kids had only six weeks to master the language and build their robots. If their first experience with an NI product had been poor, the entire project would have backfired.

However, the higher purpose of helping kids to learn rapidly and build their passion for science and technology—which could turn a light on in their young lives as well as help meet a critical educational need in the United States—fueled remarkable support from mentors, NI employees, and partners. The LabVIEW community and the platform's adoption by students exceeded the expectations of Almgren and his team many times over. "We'd hoped to get a 25 percent adoption rate," says Almgren. "We wound up with more than a 60 percent adoption rate."

Welch was not exactly known for his participative management style, but he insisted on getting the widest possible employee input, dismissing objections from executives that it wouldn't be practical to do so for a firm with hundreds of thousands of employees. The process took two years, as each draft was submitted for vigorous debate from managers at the GE training center in Crotonville, followed by further input from frontline employees through the firm's Work Out meetings. The effort was worth it, however, to create a sense of widespread ownership of the values in order to make sure they were actually followed and that people would accept vigorous measurement and enforcement. Welch gave significant credit to the new values statement for paving the way to widespread behavior changes that were critical to reforming GE's culture.

Allow Community Members to Form Subgroups to Enhance Affiliation and Relationship Building

Salesforce.com provides a good example of this strategy. The company gives customers wide latitude in running and building their communities in its Facebook-like Chatter interface, which SFDC uses to build interest for its major annual conference, Dreamforce.

After Chatter was launched, members of the site quickly made it their own, turning it into a robust "temporary" B2B community. Instead of uploading a lot of pictures, as people do on Facebook, for example, they upload PowerPoint presentations to share their ideas along with their current priorities and the most important initiatives they are working on. "We added a feature that allowed members to form specialized groups, and set up fifteen of these for them around topics like Analytics," says Tom Wong, former vice president of customer marketing.[9] "Two months before the event, members had formed another three hundred."

Rather than try to orchestrate all community activities and relationship building, Wong and his team enabled members to figure this out themselves. "We think of the Chatter interface as a bit of a matchmaking service, like Match.com," says Wong. "It provides functionality that helps the members learn about and get to know each other so *they* can decide whom to build relationships with." Some of them form noncompetitive groups that get together at Dreamforce to exchange ideas and best practices, and perhaps continue to meet afterward. Another group, formed under the title "Challenge Us," invites people to submit their hardest questions about using and leveraging the SFDC platform. "And it's most often customers who weigh in with the answers," says Wong. Another group is called "Awesome People"—who want to form a group to have fun during the four days they'll spend in San Francisco.

What's been the impact of the Chatter community on Dreamforce? Up until 2008, registrations had been growing at a robust 30 percent per year. Since then—after the recession hit and most conferences were seeing declining attendance—registrations have grown 60 percent per year until they reached 45,000 in 2011. "The only thing we did substantially differently was that we started using the Chatter platform in 2009," says Wong. "I don't know of any other explanation."

A Framework for Community Marketing

How can communities contribute to your marketing efforts? Communities can help build your brand, stimulate demand generation and sales, build awareness, spread word of mouth, and increase the speed of new product acceptance or adoption of new product releases, as well as contribute to other marketing gravity activities, such as building attendance at events or providing content for publications.

One major technology firm, for example, expects fully 10 percent of its total sales to come through its Web site by 2012, fueled by its community efforts. As we've seen earlier in this chapter, communities helped National Instruments gain significant awareness and adoption for its new robotics software, and Salesforce.com achieved substantial growth for its yearly customer conference. CSC's communities are increasing customer satisfaction, increasing product and services innovation, and strengthening the firm's brand. Since the implementation of WikonnecT, requests for new software updates have increased more than 50 percent.

To develop your own community marketing strategy, you can use the following framework to help you think it through. The main idea? Don't think small. I know of one firm that's built a customer community numbering in the hundreds of thousands—yet is satisfied with getting only 5 percent of total sales through it. Instead, think big when building community marketing efforts—like SFDC, National Instruments, and CSC are learning to do.

Create a Super Focus Group

It's a given that marketing to communities is a two-way conversation. Uncomfortable and difficult as it may be to make sense of the cacophony, embracing that fact by spending a lot of time listening can pay dividends as you get better at it. Plus, customer intelligence systems are becoming quite good at helping you make sense of the conversation relevant to you on the Web.

Citrix Systems, for example, relied heavily on community input to rapidly develop a smart phone app. The team that Chris Fleck, vice president of community and solutions development, put together believed that business users needed easy access to Microsoft business applications on their smart phones—a solution Citrix could provide. "So instead of commissioning a market research project," says Fleck, "we simply asked the question on our blog. The result was hundreds of thousands of views and hundreds of comments, many of which gave us great insight into *why* they needed it and how they would use it." Surprisingly, the most valuable comments came not from IT people but from end users such as doctors, lawyers, and small business owners, which gave the team confidence that it knew how to develop a truly useful app. A traditional market analysis would likely have resulted in a much different app that merely supported Research In Motion's BlackBerry and was completely managed by the IT department.

In the first month the new app, called Citrix Receiver, generated twenty thousand downloads and a tremendous amount of publicity and commentary on the Web. Citrix quickly took the next step, enabling the app for the iPad, and soon the combined number of downloads exceeded a million, making Citrix Receiver a top business app in the Apple App Store. Given the iPhone app success, parallel teams were established to expand to BlackBerry and Android devices. These steps quickly earned Citrix a significant presence in a rapidly expanding mobility market and provided new sales avenues for existing server infrastructure software.

Define Your Metrics: Go for Quality, Not Quantity

In the summer of 2009, Procter & Gamble (P&G) informed its media agencies that the firm was no longer paying for "eyeballs." It wanted "engagement"—which meant that getting the firm's offerings in front of millions of people would no longer cut it. P&G wanted evidence that the audiences it was paying for expressed some interest in whatever it was offering.

The same might be said for the size of your own community: would you rather have a community of hundreds of thousands who have no particular attachment to your brand or ability to do business with you, or a smaller community with high-quality members?

Most firms will have at least three types of quality members to cultivate: prospects, influencers, and customer advocates. These are the ones you want to find, measure, cultivate, grow, and engage with in your marketing efforts.[10]

- *Prospects.* These are people who match the profile of high-potential buyers for your products and services. Customer intelligence, using tools such as text analytics and surveys, is becoming increasingly adept at uncovering them for you. It makes sense to measure how many of these are participating in your communities, and then to craft engagements with them to grow that audience.

- *Influencers.* These are people whose opinions matter to your customers and prospects. As we've seen in chapter 4, Microsoft finds influencers, engages with them in community and marketing efforts, and relies on them heavily to build business in new markets. Influencers are somewhat like powerful traditional journalists or analysts in your industry, except that they are likely to *use* the product or service you sell, or that of a competitor. They thus have a higher level of credibility with buyers and can also be a significant source of insight into the direction of new product development.

Influencers aren't hard to find: start by asking your customers. Work with firms that specialize in identifying market influencers. They aren't hard to engage with either. Influencers want knowledge of the industry; your company can provide knowledge they can't get elsewhere. They want recognition and status; your company can provide it by inviting them to conferences (with a role similar to journalists, allowing them to blog). And of course they want to provide influence, and it's often a good idea to accept their input and act on it, as companies such as Microsoft with its MVP program have shown.

- *Customer advocates.* These are perhaps your most valuable source of content and conversation in your community efforts. As we've seen, peer information is the most highly valued type of information throughout the buying cycle. Whether it's through conversations in your online forums, video for your Web site, or talks and roundtables at your events, you'll want to measure and increase their presence and engagement in your community marketing efforts.

Some firms focus on building engagement with these groups, even to the point of benchmarking how many influencers they engage with versus their competition. A better thing to focus on is how well these groups are contributing to *business results* (figure 6-3). Microsoft, for example, has relatively few MVPs or influencers, but they have substantial impact on sales and branding. CSC measures the impact of its communities on how well they increase client

FIGURE 6-3

Engagement: quality versus quantity

Engagement

- Customers
- Customer *advocates*
- Prospects
- Influencers

Business Impact

- Client satisfaction
- Demand generation
- Branding
- Product development
- Product adoption
- Penetration of new markets

The goal here isn't to build big contact lists . . . the goal is to drive business results.

satisfaction, product and service innovation, and brand strength. As we've seen, Salesforce.com is well aware of the (substantial) impact its Facebook-like Chatter community has on attendance at its yearly conference. Intel looks at how well its repurposed customer reference content contributes to growth in new customer and prospect contacts through its Web and social media programs.

Learn How to Communicate Your Value Proposition as a Natural Part of the Conversation

Intel, for example, learned by experimenting how to provide customer information at appropriate times in the community's conversation—a combination of videos backed up by in-depth text, along with links to demos and other information that the community has indicated interest in.

In his widely followed blog, Hu Yoshida, the CTO of Hitachi Data Systems, mixes in specific information about HDS platform updates or strategies along with more general information of interest, such as industry trends. This works because such HDS information is important to its customers in the community and Yoshida has built enough credibility among other members that they trust that the information will be factual as well as relevant to them as well.

It's important for marketing departments to remember that the key to spreading your message and brand is the relevance and value of your message to your market—not the number and quality of influencers you can engage. Even the most powerful influencers can't (and likely won't) spread weak content.

Deploy Community Members in Your Broader Marketing Gravity Efforts

Companies such as Salesforce.com and Microsoft understand that strong community members often love the thought of engaging in what amounts to marketing efforts, even extra-community marketing efforts (figure 6-4). SFDC community members often speak or engage in panels at industry events. Microsoft's MVP influencers contribute content to white papers.

FIGURE 6-4

Communities and marketing gravity

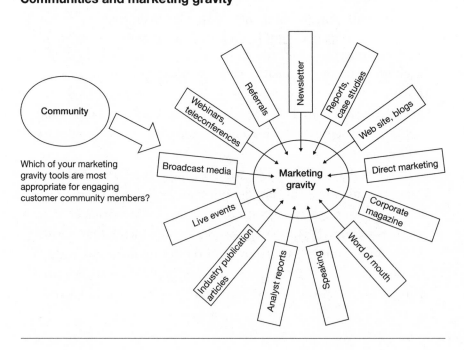

Determining the Business Value of Social Media

Regarded properly not as a strategy but as a *tool* that can contribute to community building, which in turn builds your business, social media and the Web can do a great deal:

- *Reach people you couldn't reach before—in some cases,* a lot *of people.* When Salesforce.com set up a Facebook page for its Dreamforce event (that is, a page on the Facebook site, separate from its Facebook-like Chatter page on its own site), the firm quickly got five thousand fans. The Facebook platform is extremely adept at disseminating information about people to other people. If five thousand people on Facebook like Dreamforce, are engaging with its attendee community, deciding to attend the conference, or are there, then a lot of people—including friends of the five thousand and friends of friends, and so on—are going to know about it.

- *Provide new ways to understand customers and your market.* One Holy Grail for a business is to be privy to conversations that are going on about the firm in the marketplace. What do prospects, buyers, and customers say about you to each other? For businesses whose customers are taking the conversation online and into social media, it's becoming increasingly possible to not only know and make sense of what's being said about you, but also to participate in those conversations—with substantial returns. For example, if someone on Facebook asks for recommendations for running shoes good for 5K runs in a city, it may prompt a discussion about the pros and cons of various types and brands that work best, local races or runs that are coming up, and good places to eat afterward. That can be followed by a well-targeted offer from your firm with a deal for the perfect shoe, registration for a road race coming up, and a coupon to the preferred restaurant afterward to the person asking for the referral and thirty of his friends.

- *Create new ways to provide value to your community.* Organizations that are best at extracting previously undiscovered insights from vast amounts of customer information have a huge advantage in deepening existing connections and creating new relationships. A person who takes medication for chronic conditions may be more likely to share information about relevant symptoms with medical researchers if she can do so on a patient-oriented community that she trusts.

- *Develop new ways to find people who are important to your firm.* For example, social media analytics can help you find influencers in your market and determine which are the most influential. They can also help you locate and engage with detractors of your firm. Often detractors can be turned around by establishing a connection with a human being at your firm (not, generally, in customer service!) who can answer their concerns and try to find help through outside channels if needed. Turning around such customers can create advocates for your brand, and social media tools allow you to do so inexpensively.

- *Provide new ways to build a stockpile of marketing assets.* Many companies that engage increasingly in online conversations are developing a large stockpile of favorable tweets, posts, and comments that can be turned easily into a rich source of testimonials.

The world is on the verge of an explosion in social innovation. Organizations that ride this wave successfully won't get there by focusing on social media, any more than community builders in the early twentieth century sought to master the telephone. Social media and the Web will provide valuable *tools,* but their greatest impact will be realized by companies that deploy them as part of the larger process of building vibrant communities using principles as old as human nature.

In the next chapter, we'll look at how your customers in the C suite can improve your company's strategic navigation.

Key Tasks

How Networked Customers Will Engage in Community Building with You.

Form your customers into communities—not tribes, networks, or ecosystems. Communities are far more valuable to customers and to you. To build successful customer communities:

- Remember that social media is highly useful—but it is only a tool.

- Help customers achieve high-value goals they can't achieve on their own.

- Organize around the needs and aspirations of community members, not your imperatives. At a minimum, these should include peer affiliation and the ability to build social capital, the opportunity to build reputation and status, and access to thought leadership.

- Combine individual self-interest with a higher purpose.

- Emphasize individual empowerment and shared community values.

- Embrace the emerging world of community marketing.

7

Customer-Enhanced Strategy

How C-Level Customers Can Create Rapid Growth

IF YOUR BUSINESS TYPICALLY SELLS to midlevel managers, you've likely found yourself dealing with cost-conscious buyers with little authority, limited budgets, tactical and unexciting projects, and not much potential to grow a lucrative business relationship. But if you can aim your value proposition higher—to the chiefs in the executive suite—you'll open up new worlds for your business.

How? First, senior executive buyers (also called "decision makers" for our purposes) often have broad budget authority and can make rapid buy decisions without going through corporate bureaucracy such as human resources, IT, purchasing, and so on—or worse, committees composed of such groups. (See table 7-1.)

Second, the hidden wealth of senior executive customers—the value *beyond* what they purchase—can be extraordinary. C-level executives can make superb advocates, influencers, and contributors for your business:

TABLE 7-1

ROI on customer programs for decision makers (DMs)

Companies that engage with executive customers reap substantial rewards.

	With DM program	Little or no DM program
Retention	90%	70%
Account growth rate	12%	4%
Referenceable	94%	28%

Source: Geehan Group Research and Sean Geehan, *The B2B Executive Playbook: How Winning B2B Companies Achieve Sustainable, Predictable & Profitable Growth* (Cincinnati, OH: Clerisy Press, 2011.)

- C-level executives almost always have extensive professional networks, including peers in similar positions at other organizations—a great ongoing relationship with one can open many doors over a period of years.

- For B2B firms in particular, just a few of these relationships can result in substantial additional business—in some cases, they can constitute the lion's share of corporate profits. A typical $2 billion business-to-customer firm might have a couple of million customers. A $2 billion B2B firm might have a few hundreds of customers—and forty of those might account for 70 percent of its business.

- C-level customers can provide access to their corporate strategy deliberations, which can provide invaluable information guiding your own strategic direction to ensure you continue creating and expanding the value you provide to their business.

- Relationships with the C suite can lead to codesign or co-innovation programs, in which joint working teams can pour concrete over such strategic initiatives, turning them into reality at the product or service level.

- As your importance to such customers increases, *your* success becomes increasingly important to them. They want you to have the success and funding that comes with it to continue to innovate and help their business succeed.

- Other value-creating opportunities that C-level relationships can create include tapping into the executives' influence and standing in the industry, manifested in speaking on your behalf or touting your service in industry publications or events as they relate the ways in which you're helping their business to succeed. They can be gold-standard customer references.

During the 2008–2009 recession, Harris Broadcast delivered superior performance relative to its market and competitors. Former president Tim Thorsteinson credits its executive customer engagement efforts. For example, members of the firm's executive advisory board, who accounted for 16 percent of the firm's revenue at the time, provided input that enabled the firm to rapidly revamp its product line: 50 percent of its current line in 2009 was developed in the previous twenty-four months. Overall, its executive customer engagement efforts achieved the following results:

- Increased sales slightly, despite the recession

- Improved margins as well as predictability of sales

- Increased senior management's confidence in the business trajectory and forecasts

- Created better market alignment and higher stakeholder returns

Although getting access to the C suite may seem daunting, more companies can make the connection to these executives than you might think. Among other things, top executives today confront increasingly swift market transformations, increasing technological complexity, and profound changes in how they engage with their own customers, manage volatility and risk, and improve innovation and new product development. All of this points to an increased openness at the C level to new ideas and relationships.

In this chapter you'll learn how to go about getting a seat at the executive suite table, including the following:

- How to understand the agenda of the C suite and provide solutions that address that agenda.

- How to determine whether your products and services are, in fact, making an impact that's important to the C suite—and how to increase your ability to do so.

- How companies without clear access to the C suite can get it—sometimes with the help of existing, lower-level customer advocates in the same organization.

- How to determine whether your organization is ready to make that transition, and what you need to do to get it ready.

- And, of course, how to tap the huge reserves of hidden wealth such customers can bring to your firm.

When to Pursue the C Suite: You're Sexier Than You Think

Developing relationships and building a business portfolio with C-level buyers requires a special mind-set, in addition to the ability to deliver. In a phrase, you and your staff must be able to achieve the status of trusted adviser or even trusted partner with the executive buyer. That means knowing how you can contribute clearly and substantially to his or her success.

Learn the C-Level Executive's Agenda

What follows are some typical high-priority items for senior executives.[1] Can you make an impact on one or more? Think about it carefully—you might surprise yourself.

- *Growing revenue.* Can you connect your offerings to increases in the customer's top-line growth? If so, you'll gain the attention of senior management.

- *Cutting costs.* Alternatively, can you demonstrably help the customer to cut costs? Particularly in tough economic times, even relatively small savings might get the attention of the C suite—even at a $100 billion firm. As Cardinal Health CIO Patty Morrison puts it, "Don't be afraid of saving just $5,000, $10,000, or $50,000. Even when I was at Motorola, I was interested in that kind of money because budgets were very tight."

- *Reinventing customer relationships.* This is increasingly a C-suite issue. Customers are demanding better products and services from businesses that actually help them meet their goals, as well as more honest dialogue. They also want access to peer interaction. Senior executives increasingly realize this and are looking for ways to get customers much more involved in the actual processes of the business.[2] If you can help them do so, C-level executives will want to talk to you.

- *Achieving technological superiority.* Increasingly, top executives want to know the following: Are we keeping current? Are our systems gaining real insights into customers, markets, and our competitors from all the data that's out there? Is the product or service you are selling keeping us ahead of our competitors or causing us to lag?

- *Improving innovation and new product development.* Companies in many industries also consider innovation a C suite issue. They know they must develop attractive new products and services to keep up with rapidly changing customer needs as well as stiff competition. In many industries, the success of new product and solution development efforts remains abysmal.[3]

- *Managing volatility.* Volatility—unpredictable and rapidly changing business conditions—is the new normal. Businesses

Is Your Organization Ready for C-Level Relationships?

You and your executive team may be keen for such relationships, but you'll need your organization behind you. Some questions to ask yourself first:

- What percentage of their time are your executives spending (or willing to spend) with customers? Ten percent is not good. Thirty percent is better.

- Are customer issues discussed regularly and in depth in your executive meetings? Are solutions developed and followed up?

- Which conversation is more likely to occur at your firm during product development planning: "If we can get 20 percent of our customers to buy the new offering, it will increase revenues by 8 percent" or "The new offering will help customers cut time-to-market by 15 percent, pay for itself within the first year, and address one of the top concerns they've expressed to us and talked about in their own executive forums"? That last approach will serve the C suite best.

- Do you have dedicated relationship managers for your high-value, C-level customers? These are folks who make sure that the issues

are accepting that they can't wait it out; that volatility is here to stay. Can you help them manage or thrive or perhaps even exploit this volatility to their advantage? That's a C-suite issue.

- *Gaining mastery over complexity.* Complexity and its unintended consequences are haunting corporate performance. For example, increasingly sophisticated hardware and software systems are often cobbled together from a variety of manufacturers. How do you get these systems working seamlessly to deliver the overall result companies want—that is, how do you ensure they're interoperable? It's a complexity issue that can be critical to an organization's performance.

they raise get addressed, that the necessary work to follow up on them gets done, and that someone communicates this to the customer.

- Do relationship managers offer senior executive customers a full range of opportunities to engage with you, by participating in any or all of your reference programs, industry events, advisory boards, cobranding or codevelopment efforts, and the like?

- Do your senior executives and relationship managers know what it takes for your key customers' firms to succeed? Do they understand how your firm is helping them to do so?

- Do your company policies actually reflect and reinforce customer centricity throughout the organization? It leaves a bad taste in the mouth of an executive when your people are treating his people poorly—that can pour very cold water on the warmest relationship you've labored to establish.

- Do you have processes to measure the ongoing health of the relationship?

If you can help solve it, you can get a seat at the C-level table. We'll see how Microsoft is doing just that later in this chapter.

In addition to such business issues, it's also important to get to know the personal agendas of C-level customers as you build the relationship—these are key to knowing their emotional drivers. Are they focused on building their career further, or on building their relationships and their network? Perhaps building personal wealth drives them, or increasing their influence in their industry or profession. Or perhaps they're becoming passionate about giving back, contributing to their community, mentoring young people. Any of these can be tremendous emotional drivers—and if you can provide help or guidance, you'll find that phone calls get returned quickly and the relationship will warm up rapidly.

Can *You* Pull It Off?

Once you begin to uncover your C-level prospect's agenda, the next obvious question is, Can you help her achieve it in some significant way? There are a couple of things to remember here. First, don't brush aside too quickly your ability to contribute—even saving $5,000 per year in costs can get the attention of a prominent CIO such as Patty Morrison. As she explains, the key is to build a *relationship* that offers the C-suite executive a full range of opportunities to engage with you. Don't show up only when you need a reference.[4] (See the sidebar "Is Your Organization Ready for C-Level Relationships?")

Second, developing such relationships needs to be an ongoing process. Regular touch points—perhaps an e-mail every three or four weeks pointing out a business article of high interest to the customer, lunch two or three times a year, and the like—are essential. Part of the value you can provide here might be connections to peers that you know would be interesting and useful, or perhaps an industry conference where the executive could speak. Ultimately, of course, you need to provide impact to the executive's business agenda.

The sidebar "How National Instruments Gains Access to the C Suite" illustrates how one engineering software firm, mired in selling products to midlevel buyers, moved beyond that to selling higher-margin solutions to more senior executives. Notice how NI's *existing* midlevel customers helped it gain access to senior levels—a particularly creative example of how its customers provide value beyond what they purchase.

If your company is accustomed to selling strictly to midlevel buyers, as National Instruments was, you too may be able to use this to your advantage when it comes to gaining access to senior decision makers. A carefully thought-out approach can turn these midlevel buyers into a much stronger asset than might be first apparent.

How National Instruments Gains Access to the C Suite

For companies that already have a robust customer reference program, an obvious place to begin is to extract benchmark financial impact information from existing case studies. For companies accustomed to selling to midlevel buyers, however, the case studies likely focus on strictly technical features. That was the case at National Instruments.

When the company began a process to pursue C-suite customers, its more than six hundred existing case studies showed things like how NI software could power robots, measure the flow rate of diesel nozzles, and the like. These had to change to "business impact" studies in which the writers extracted information such as reductions in total cost of ownership, improvements in productivity and time-to-market efficiencies, and overall financial savings, as well as improvements to return on investment and payback periods resulting from NI products and solutions.

Most customers didn't have the ability to generate such numbers, so NI took that responsibility, creating a senior, cross-functional team to do so, in partnership with customers. Their goal: development of "business impact case studies" (BICS). The NI team crafted the following process to create the BICS.

NI's Five-Step Process to Get to the C Suite

1. Identify the best candidate customers who have potentially realized the greatest financial impact, and reach out to them.

2. Align the business case study efforts—working through existing midlevel customers as much as possible—to locate the appropriate executive director or vice president at the target customer to sponsor the initiative. Ask this executive to help identify senior employees in his or her organization who can provide a complete picture of financial and business impacts.

3. Engage by conducting 360-degree interviews with the senior employees identified by the customer sponsor. The NI team would

(*continued*)

How National Instruments Gains Access to the C Suite (*continued*)

allocate an hour for such interviews over a period of one to two days.

4. Analyze the resulting data to build a financial model for the customer's before-and-after financial scenarios, generate the business productivity and financial impact numbers, and identify the customer's business challenge together with the solution that the NI platform provides. This information, along with supporting quotes from senior executives, becomes the new BICS.

5. Finalize the case study by sharing it with the customer, validating the financial impact numbers, obtaining and incorporating feedback, and getting necessary approvals. Publish it.

Such case studies opened doors to the C suite at prospective new customers by showing how they could derive powerful business benefits from NI solutions. As Dr. Sugato Deb, director of strategic development at NI, put it: "Senior executives are typically hungry for this level of business and industry insight, and very few suppliers provide that." In addition, Deb and his team found they were getting into extended and open conversations with executives. "We were focusing on creating business impact on a large scale. Our previous attempts to reach this level of customer and hold such conversations were much more challenging without such business insights."

Engage with Customers to Improve Your Strategic Impact

To continue the momentum that a well-planned business impact case study effort can create, you can form customer advisory boards (CABs) from the groups of customers who have excelled in realizing business value. You'll have a compelling value proposition: the chance to exchange ideas and develop best practices with peers who are also excelling. Of course, they'll also want to interact with *you* and provide guidance on developing new solutions to address additional issues.

The NI team formed such boards and combined the rich information they provided with its own expertise built up over years, resulting in the development of best practice themes and scorecards. The team worked with its CABs to determine which competencies—strategic, organizational, employee skills, process skills, and the like—its customer firms would need in order to achieve the financial gains possible from using NI products and services. NI then created a business group to deliver the new services that arose from these conversations and to grow the number of such engagements.

The result: NI emerged with a clear picture of the business value its customers were already receiving, an understanding of how its star customers were reaping the highest financial returns, a well-defined "best practices map" that other customers could use to help achieve such results, content-rich training tools that sales could use to engage in discussions with prospective executives about achieving such returns, and, of course, some very powerful sales collateral to leave behind or publish on its Web site, social media sites, or through other media.

Over the past few years, NI has seen its large-orders revenue grow at more than twice the rate of the company's overall revenue growth. This additional revenue is fueling most of the company's present expansion.

To get started on this journey, a firm needs a process to achieve four things:

1. Uncover whatever financial and strategic impact your products and services are already producing for current customers.

2. Determine *how* your star customers—those who may *already* be obtaining such higher-level results—are doing so.

What are their essential competencies that make such results possible? This will provide a foundation for defining best practices. Note that it will generally be easy to recruit these performers to help in the effort: after all, you're creating documentation that will show how successful they've been.

3. Find *recommenders* or *advocates* from among your current lower-level customers who have access to the C suite or to other decision makers with large budgets.

4. To help them make the case for you, *document* the best practices of these star performers. Look especially for best practices that reach beyond just the technological benefits of your products and include the strategic process that *customers* follow to deploy your technology, as well as the business impact generated.

By the way, such documentation will serve a second important purpose. You'll use it to train your account managers to sell such business benefits to senior-level buyers—rather than the product features they're used to selling to lower-level buyers. And, of course, such documentation can be done in the form of case studies for use in closing actual deals.

Developing C-Level Relationships with Increasing Reciprocal Value

Because customer relationships can be difficult and unpredictable, many businesses regard them as a chore or a necessary evil. Yet the customer relationship is the most fundamental relationship in business—indeed, in our capitalist culture. At its heart, it can be one of the most exciting—if approached correctly. At its best, it represents a mutual exchange of value in which both sides are helping each other succeed. At the same time, it satisfies our deep needs to grow ourselves, as well as our desire to help others. It should be a source of immense satisfaction.

If that is not your experience, then you have the wrong customers, you're not providing significant value yourself, or you're not harvesting full value from your customers in return. This is particularly so with C-level customers: they have much to offer. It's an exciting world when you enter into C-level relationships. Senior executives tend to be bright, highly engaged not just in their businesses but also the world around them, intellectually curious and well informed, often widely read, with passionate pursuits outside of business that they love to explore (or *would* love to if they had the time). They're fun to hang around with. If you cultivate enough of them—and it doesn't take that many—they can ensure the prosperity of your business.

One caveat: Don't get hung up on pursuing C-level *titles.* Sometimes highly influential executives with large, discretionary budgets will have nondescript titles that provide no indication of the power they wield. You don't want to overlook such people. At the same time, some executives with titles that sound high powered wield very little influence or budget. That's why it's important to cultivate relationships with employees at your customers who know the ins and outs of their organization and can provide you with access to the *real* powers that be.

The sidebar "The Company–Customer Relationship" illustrates the typically static way that most companies view their customer exchanges versus a much more expanded, fulfilling view.

To illustrate the concept of increasing reciprocal value, let me offer the example of one of my own new-client relationships. The client is a talented executive who had recently taken a marketing position at a global technology firm. Her business goals included energizing her new team to make a quick and significant impact on the performance of the marketing organization. Her *personal* goals included continuing to grow her career in marketing and, in particular, customer engagement and business development. To that end, she hoped to grow her network and raise her visibility in the appropriate professional communities.

I began by engaging her and her team in a day-and-a-half workshop that got the team energized and focused on three exciting,

The Company–Customer Relationship

The following figure illustrates how many companies look at their customer relationships, even their C-level relationships.

A static value relationship

While products and services may change, the value relationship doesn't.

Here's a better approach: *increasing reciprocal value*, in this case for an executive customer who wants to build his business's revenues and whose personal goals include increasing his professional visibility and reputation.

Increasing reciprocal value

Both sides' contribution of value continues to grow.

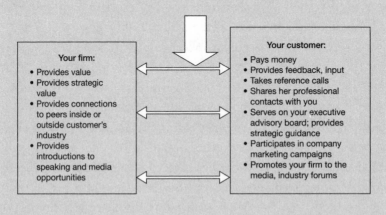

high-value goals. As I followed up later to guide the team toward significant progress in implementation, the client and I developed a trusted adviser relationship. Based on what I learned about her personal and professional goals, we created a video testimonial, co-presented a teleconference together, worked on a case study for this book, and along the way provided mutual introductions for each other to our networks as appropriate. On a personal level, it's been exciting for both of us to help each other succeed and grow in the process.

Next we'll look at how you can leverage a key aspect of reciprocal value from your C-level customer contributors.

Forming a C-Level Industry Council: You Have More Clout Than You Think

Forming an industry council of C-level executives is a daunting prospect. Attracting high-performing executives, working the logistics to get them together, holding their attention, and providing a serious impact on them and their businesses might seem like too much of a hill to climb. But more companies can pull this off than think they can. The rewards in terms of thought leadership, branding, and stature in your industry make it worth considering. In addition, running such a council is not as expensive as one might think.

Determine: Can You Do It?

Start by taking one of the major C-level issues identified earlier in this chapter and ask: Can we plausibly help executives address this, at least in part? And would we be willing and able to work with other organizations, including competitors if necessary, to solve important problems raised by the council?

Microsoft established an executive customer council about six years ago precisely by doing this. One of the major issues faced by CIOs for more than a decade—and one that won't be going away any time soon—is getting their increasingly complex technology systems, from a variety of vendors, to work smoothly together.

That compelling issue, plus the participation of several respected IT executives, created the foundation for Microsoft's Interoperability Executive Customer (IEC) Council. Today the IEC Council gathers some forty or so senior technology executives representing global organizations and governments twice each year. Its purpose is to evaluate and provide input into Microsoft's interoperability efforts. Microsoft taps this group for input and dialogue on topics ranging from the company's own product plans and partnerships to participation in industry standards and open source development projects and to emerging industry trends and customer priorities. Representatives on the council include CIOs, CTOs, and other senior systems architects from large, well-known global organizations in the public and private sectors. The entire group benefits from the consistent participation of its membership. By now, as trust has grown over the years, IEC Council members open up to each other and Microsoft in remarkable ways, as we'll see in a moment.

It's Not About Your Resources; It's About the Peers You Can Attract

"But we're not Microsoft," you might say. "We can't command their resources or their reputation." In fact, industry councils aren't that expensive to run: they require executive leadership to drive them and relatively inexpensive resources for the logistics and follow-up coordination. Several members of Microsoft's IEC Council have said that the two primary selling points for their participation are the simple model of the forum, which encourages outside perspectives, and the direct access they have to their peers.

Note that it's not the organizer's clout and visibility that draws people: it's the quality of the *peers* that you can attract, plus whether the time spent participating on the council will reap generous results that draw executives. Several years ago, a young man of whom few people had heard established the Global 50, which became a highly successful forum for CEOs of major corporations. He had little money and no reputation, but he did have connections to a few highly attractive (i.e., influential) CEOs, plus a convincing model that participation would result in significant benefits. That's what attracted the rest.

Realizing the Rewards of Industry Leadership

Spending quality personal "face time" with a room full of senior executive buyers from top organizations in attractive target markets allows one to gain deep insights into everything from their business concerns to their strategic direction, their personal agendas, industry information and insight, and more that wouldn't be available anywhere else. The rewards of gaining industry leadership through establishing an industry council should speak for themselves.

- *Expanding your industry knowledge and your network.* For example, Wells Fargo has built senior executive advisory councils in a number of industries. These aren't industry councils (they consist only of Wells Fargo customers), but they nonetheless provide invaluable industry information. "Our transportation council provides us with insights into that industry, and as a result, insights into our customers' perspectives, that we just couldn't get anywhere else," says Steve Ellis, executive vice president of wholesale services.

  In addition, as your council grows, you gain the benefit of a virtuous circle effect: your network of senior leaders grows, which increases your ability to connect executives to other attractive peers, increasing your value to them dramatically.

- *Building your thought leadership.* What's more, the information a firm develops from collaborations with and between prestigious and influential council members can place it in a strong position of thought leadership on issues of high importance to the industry. Microsoft, for example, is busily building on that concept by creating interoperable products and technologies, along with thought leadership to grow

industry awareness of the issue and encourage more cooperation from other vendors across the industry.

- *Enhancing your reputation and brand.* Perhaps the greatest benefit to your firm is that, by playing well in the sand-
  box, so to speak, you can create goodwill for your brand
  image. Microsoft has done this through the IEC Council by
  publically addressing an important industry issue in precisely the way that industry leaders would want to have it
  addressed: by looking at *all* critical aspects—not just the
  ones that Microsoft itself can develop solutions for—and
  bringing in whatever resources it can, including other vendors, to solve problems on behalf of customers. This is true
  trusted adviser status, and Microsoft has achieved it—not
  just with individual customers but en masse in its industry.

  To date, Microsoft's IEC Council members have identified some fifty key areas in which improved interoperability
  between their systems was needed, a majority of which have
  been resolved. For those issues too complex to be addressed
  through this forum, Microsoft is seeking ways in which it
  can bring other vendors and relevant organizations into the
  solution. In such ways, the firm has placed itself in a superb
  position to establish leadership and its long-term commit-
  ment to an important industry issue, and to foster openness
  in its efforts to help address it.

Making an Industry Council Work

To pull together and keep together such a high-influence group of
executive customers that can provide this kind of value to Microsoft, the firm must deliver exceptional value as well (figure 7-1).
Here's how Microsoft does so.

- *Determine major needs this community has—without
  regard to your business offerings.* Interoperability—getting
  technology systems to work in a complex, heterogeneous
  environment—is a significant problem for CIOs. Many of

FIGURE 7-1

How Microsoft gets results from its Interoperability Executive Customer Council

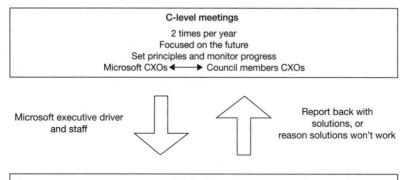

C-level meetings

2 times per year
Focused on the future
Set principles and monitor progress
Microsoft CXOs ◄———► Council members CXOs

Microsoft executive driver
and staff

Report back with
solutions, or
reason solutions won't work

Work stream

Ongoing meetings and interaction
Focused on developing solutions and implementation
Senior IT representatives appointed by main council members
Microsoft's senior IT reps ◄———►Council members' senior IT reps

them have appealed to technology vendors for help in addressing the issue; the need was clearly there. Microsoft made the decision to demonstrate leadership by taking steps to actively address these concerns.

- *Ask, "Can we address it? Does it make strategic sense to do so?"* One reason it made sense for Microsoft to take on this challenge was to build its reputation for addressing an important industry need in a collaborative way.

- *Appoint an executive driver.* Executive participation needs to go beyond sponsorship—-someone who offers support and makes the occasional appearance. You'll need a driver who gets heavily involved in meetings, and in follow-up. Follow-up includes having an internal structure under the executive driver's control that gets things done (see the next point).

- *Build parallel working groups to implement projects.* This is key. It does no good to meet, brainstorm, and develop exciting projects with senior executives unless the projects turn into actions and results. Microsoft developed six working groups, composed of implementation people from both IEC Council members' firms and Microsoft. The Microsoft working group members report to the executive driver. Failing to follow up is not an option.

- *Report back from the first.* As mentioned earlier, in its first few years, the Microsoft IEC Council identified about fifty "scenarios," or technology and business issues resulting from interoperability failures. Almost all were addressed and solved: Microsoft has declined to pursue only a few— and communicates its decisions on why or why not to its members. As the IEC Council continues into its sixth year, the dialogue among council members today has evolved to address longer-range planning scenarios, touching on topics such as the consumerization of IT, systems management, virtualization, and the cloud.

- *Learn.* To gain more clout in the interoperability movement, Microsoft is sponsoring white papers and other publications on the subject based on its work with the IEC Council, in order to grow industry awareness and encourage more cooperation from skeptical vendors. It has also figured out how council members can engage more closely and influence senior Microsoft executives in ways that create substantial mutual value for both.

In a complex, hyperconnected world, C-level executives must constantly be open to new solutions. More companies, including possibly yours, can address those executives' challenges than think they can. The rewards for doing so are immense: buyers who can make fast decisions and aren't as budget constrained as the midlevel customers you've been dealing with—*if* you can deliver the value they need—and substantive contributors to your marketing strategy, among other things.

Next we'll examine how customers can help you make dramatic improvements in your new product development.

Key Tasks

Engaging C-Level Customers for Rapid Growth.

- If you're not already selling to the C suite, consider doing so. More firms can do this than think they can.

- Determine whether your products and services appeal—or could appeal—to senior executive buyers.

- To gain access to senior executive buyers, work with select, existing midlevel customers who (1) recognize the strategic potential of your offerings and (2) can help you gain access to their C suite.

- Form a team to work with such customers to develop the data showing any strategic impact you're already achieving and to brainstorm ways to dramatically enhance such impact.

- In the process of doing so, start reaching out to senior executives who would be interested in the results, and engage with them in the project.

- Document these results with business impact case studies, and use these to show senior executives at existing customers, as well as prospects, how you can provide value to them.

8

The Most Innovative Designers

How to Get Meaningful Customer Input to Make Dramatic Improvements in New Product Development

INNOVATION IS DIFFICULT. Some published estimates place the failure rate of new product introductions between 40 percent and 75 percent.[1] That's hardly a surprise, since the typical process used for product innovation seems to defy logic.

Think about it: Product marketing groups attempt to understand emerging customer needs through market research, focus groups, and customer interviews. That information is then passed on to R&D departments that attempt to turn it into useful or even breakthrough new products. However, customers are notoriously unable to articulate their emerging needs, and even when they can, a company's internal product developers rarely gain real insight into what customers value or even how they use the products they buy—which is particularly true at firms that have complex products being sold to a variety of customers with heterogeneous needs.[2] (See "*Do* You Understand Your Customers? A Diagnostic.")

Do You Understand Your Customers? A Diagnostic

Few executives would say that they and their firms don't understand their customers. A good idea is to assess your abilities as an innovator. Here's a quick diagnostic:

1. We're often surprised by how our customers use our products.

2. We're not regarded as innovative in our industry.

3. Our efforts to innovate are *reactive*. We're following rather than leading the way.

4. Too often we scramble to keep up with hot new technologies that turn out to be duds.

5. We're not coming up with breakthrough products.

6. We're overly dependent on acquisitions to develop new and break-through solutions.

Truth be told, most firms (even Apple) would answer "yes" to question 1. It's a plus if you at least work to determine how customers are actually using your product and services, even if you assume you know. But if you find yourself answering "yes" to more than two or three of the rest of the list, particularly questions 4, 5, or 6, then you are seriously out of touch with customer needs.

And yet, the demand for better, more innovative products is only going up among buyers who have increasing knowledge and access to alternatives. Buyers expect the companies with which they do business to provide products and services that reflect a better understanding of their needs.[3] No wonder that many firms rely on acquisitions to bolster their ability to provide new and break-through innovations. Let the market winnow out the best new applications and technologies. Of course, the problem is that acquiring companies have to pay a hefty premium for these assets, and often overpay.

Despite their frequent inability to articulate what they want, some customers can provide a superb source of innovative new products and services. In previous chapters, we've focused mainly on uncovering the *advocacy* and *influence* parts of the hidden wealth that customers can create for you. Now we'll take a look at the *contribution* they can provide, the "C" in their AIC activities. We'll see how such contributions can create dramatic ROR for your firm, and tremendous reciprocal value for customers, who finally get products and services that meet their needs superbly.

There are two broad ways to tap this valuable ROR. First, your customers have things—information, knowledge, resources, even the urge to affiliate—that other customers want and will pay for, sometimes handsomely. The following section offers a framework for thinking through how you might enable those kinds of innovative exchanges to happen. Second, certain customers may well be better at innovating than you are, and are often happy to share their designs with you—an insight that revolutionized innovation at a firm, 3M, whose prowess in innovation is legendary. We will explore what that concept can mean for your company's ability to develop groundbreaking products and services, and then we'll look at 3M's story.

A Framework for Tapping the Hidden Value of Customer Communities

Although it can be frustrating to try to figure out what customers really want, there's one thing that they almost certainly want at some time or other, and in some cases are willing to pay handsomely for: stuff from other customers. As companies grow their customer communities and connect them to each other through the Web (if the customers haven't already done so themselves), they can tap this vein. Very often, they find that customers in a community setting are willing and even eager to make remarkable contributions that create considerable value to other customers and to their business. Following is a framework for tapping the value of your community.

What Would Customers Like to Learn from Each Other?

A good model for thinking about this question comes from the book-buying world. Book buyers want to know, for example, what other readers, particularly readers "like me," thought of a book they're considering buying. Amazon.com provides this information through its customer star-ratings system in which buyers can rate, review, and comment on books they've read. Amazon.com also allows reviewers to upload their profile so that buyers can understand more about the reviewers whose reviews they're reading—and locate reviewers who are "like me."

Amazon.com also has a system to *rate the reviewers,* allowing the buyer to gain a sense of who are the good reviewers. Another example of powerful customer-generated content is recommendations for other books, generated by increasingly sophisticated software showing what other customers "like me" are also buying. As a regular book buyer on Amazon.com, I can tell you that often these recommendations uncannily come up with suggestions I had indeed been thinking about buying, reinforcing that impulse.

What Valuable Data Contained in the Community Can We Marshal?

The legal research and information firm Westlaw has developed a superb—and lucrative—service for its law firm customers. The firm has traditionally provided legal research services for its clients. But as its community has grown, the firm realized that its law firm clients in particular were interested in information about the legal business, and in particular were interested in how they and the markets they served stacked up to other firms and markets. So Westlaw created Peer Monitor, which aggregates anonymous data on firms' financial and operational performance, collected from participating clients. That allows participating clients to benchmark such things as staffing levels and performance as well as conduct market analysis when considering whether to begin a new practice or open an office in a new region. The service has proven quite profitable for Westlaw.

What Resources Does the Community Have That We Could Access?

Skype, for example, has built a good-quality, global communications firm that transmits voice and video, with virtually no capital investment. The basic service (including voice and video) is free and reaches everyone in the world with access to a computer and the Internet. Revenue comes from add-on services such as voice mail, as well as calls that customers make to mobile phones and land lines. How did the company create an infrastructure that can handle the millions of calls its customers make simultaneously at any particular time? By using the idle power on callers' PCs. When you place a call on Skype, you're using your own computing power to manage the call.

What Information Might the Community Provide That We Can Harvest?

Salesforce.com, Dell, Starbucks, and others have used communities to tackle the tough issue of what features and functionality should be added to existing products and services. This is a hard question to answer, particularly for a widely heterogeneous customer base that has different needs, different perspectives, and lots of requests. There's only so much a company can do, only so much it can understand about its customer base. Therefore Salesforce.com and the others let their communities decide, through such mechanisms as SFDC's IdeaExchange—a software interface that helps product developers understand, group, and prioritize the tens of thousands of feature requests it gets from customers. Such a process helps companies like SFDC and Dell determine which requests are the ones people want most, and also makes it likely that customers will continue to provide input.

A transparent process that allows the community to choose has a number of benefits. For one thing, the community is likely to arrive at a better answer regarding where to devote your scarce product development resources than you would have. For another, it satisfies customers clamoring to know why *their* suggested change wasn't implemented, when the question is proposed to hundreds or thousands of people and very few agree.

How Would Our Community Members Like to Engage with Each Other?

Experienced professionals, for example, love to mentor young people. National Instruments built on that fact to promote and build awareness of its little-known LabVIEW software, while also creating customers of the future. As part of its community-building efforts, the firm matched experienced robotics engineers in mentoring relationships with student contestants.

Both Procter & Gamble and Unilever have nurtured communities in which female customers can share experiences in meaningful ways beyond the products they buy. P&G originally designed its BeingGirl community for teens and preteens to promote its feminine hygiene products, since traditional TV and print ads make them uncomfortable. At first, the site disseminated content only from experts, which did little to build attachment. When it began establishing forums in which young women at a sensitive time in their lives could share experiences, form connections, and have some fun in the process, the community took off—it now gets 400,000 unique visitors per month. Of course, the young women share and ask questions on a variety of topics, but in such a trusting atmosphere, it's much easier for the firm to discreetly and effectively promote its Always and Tampax brands as well as partner brands. P&G finds that such advertising is four times more effective than TV ads.

What Services Might the Community Offer Its Members?

It's become commonplace for firms to gradually offload service needs to customer communities. However, communities can generate surprisingly sophisticated information and support. Some executives balk at the notion that uncredentialed nonexperts can create reliable information, but a threshold regarding that misconception was crossed several years ago by *Wikipedia*. Anyone can submit or modify articles to the online encyclopedia. Over time, some restrictions and rules have emerged—but always created and agreed to by the self-same community of amateurs. A study by the scientific journal *Nature* concluded that information on *Wikipedia* is just as likely to be accurate as the expert-created *Encyclopaedia Britannica*. And it goes without saying, *Wikipedia* covers far more subjects and contains far more information than a closed publication like the *Britannica* ever could.

Intuit has leveraged this phenomenon in its TurboTax product. TurboTax now contains a button right on the program that a customer preparing taxes can push if she has a question about tax regulations or gets stuck in her preparation. The button takes her to a community of other TurboTax customers, where she can immediately pose her question. Some executives at Intuit were wary, in part because of the nonexpert issue, or "the blind leading the blind." But large community dynamics are powerful sources of accurate information and knowledge. Intuit's internal tax experts reviewed and confirmed the quality of the answers generated by the community, as incorrect information was quickly corrected, and correct answers were refined as additional answers came in. Within five weeks of the launch of the community, one-third of the questions that customers had posed had answers.

Who Else Can We Add to the Community to Create Value?

Threadless, an online firm that manufactures and sells T-shirts, puts volunteer designers and artists together with customers in a community: the designers submit designs, and the customers select those that Threadless puts into production. The designers receive $2,500 plus a royalty for any design that's picked, and in any case get free exposure for their work. Threadless gets inexpensive art work, plus market research as well as buy-in from customers who see and vote on the T-shirts and buy them up quickly when they're released, a process that also reduces inventory levels.

Beyond such contributions, certain customers have both the knowledge and willingness to actively *participate* in the product development process—and advances in technology are making this easier.

Transforming Your Customers into Innovators

Many firms are rethinking their businesses less as providers of internally created products and services and more as *platforms* that allow customers to create their own experience and value. Such firms are achieving the ideal of giving customers what they want, when, where, and how they want it. Social media and the Internet, of course, are rapidly creating many of the tools to help do this. Let's look at four key steps that organizations can take to move toward this ideal, followed by a discussion of how to bring customers into the design process and the story of how 3M did it.

Four Steps to Making Your Company a Design Platform

1. Let Customers Create Their Own Experience
Even Apple, known for a culture under Steve Jobs that famously resisted allowing customers or outside developers to alter any of its platforms, finally bowed to a growing reality. The company simply didn't have the resources to satisfy, or even understand, all the significant customer needs that arose for iPod and iPad users. However, a lot of people *outside* the firm—including the customers with

those needs—were willing to modify Apple's product or service to meet them. So Apple created an Apps Store and is enjoying a 30 percent cut of the sales, which now number in the hundreds of thousands, while its customers enjoy an increasingly rich and customized experience on its iPhone and iPad platforms.

The ability to make it easy for customers to alter products to better meet their needs is not confined to software firms. Mid-tech, low-tech, and no-tech firms have been doing the same thing for a long time with enablers such as toolkits or modular products that allow add-ons and customization. International Flavors and Fragrances (IFF), for example, which provides specialty flavors to the food industry around the world, provides a toolkit that allows customers to modify flavors for themselves. GE provides customers with tools on its Web site that allow them to design plastic products that better meet their needs.

Discount furniture maker IKEA engages customers in assembling their own furniture, a process that allows them to customize as well. Research has shown that by doing so, some customers develop a particularly strong connection with the company. Some are even moved to write songs praising the company and to volunteer to live in the store. In one study, researchers asked college students to assemble an IKEA storage box, and then report how much they would pay to take it home. Those who assembled the box were, surprisingly, willing to pay *more* for the boxes and were happier with them than those who didn't do their own assembly.

2. Build Communities Around the Customer Cocreation Process

A few years ago, construction toy maker LEGO worked with engineers at MIT to develop software and motor inserts that would allow customers to propel the toys they built with the firm's building blocks. In effect, customers could now build robots. When launched, the product was a solid hit, but then something quite unexpected happened. Within weeks, some one thousand outsiders had hacked into the software and, further, were forming communities on their own to exchange code. To many firms this would represent a product and intellectual property nightmare. (Sony encountered a similar response to its new line of robots, and immediately began filing lawsuits.)

But executives at LEGO realized that the changes the hackers were making represented major improvements. So did other customers. Therefore the firm decided to support their efforts. Today the community of users numbers in the tens of thousands and has developed an amazing array of robots—far beyond anything that the firm's seven internal developers could have come up with, and that's no criticism of the developers. As MIT engineer Eric von Hippel wryly commented, "I'm from MIT so I can do the math. A thousand is a lot more than seven."

As a result, LEGO has repositioned itself. Somewhat like Salesforce.com's transition from a software company to a platform company, LEGO now regards itself not as a toy maker but as a toy *publisher.* Its entire product line and software constitute a toolkit, or platform, allowing the most creative customers to create the toys they really want rather than having to make do with what corporate product developers decide they should have.

3. Rethink Your Core Competencies

This kind of evaluation is important, particularly if your company serves a rapidly growing market with a large, heterogeneous customer base. It makes little sense to depend on a few internal product development specialists to understand such a market. Rather, like marketing and sales professionals are doing, product developers for such markets will increasingly be judged by how well they bring customers into the development process. That will not only create a much more robust customer experience, but also will allow companies to divert resources into areas where internal process experts *can* add value that outsiders cannot—such as production and distribution.

Indeed, Salesforce.com has embraced the concept of having its customers as well as outside developers create apps so thoroughly that it has refashioned its offering from "software as a service" (SaaS) to "*platform* as a service" (PaaS). This grew out of the firm's recognition that its developers couldn't possibly keep up with the needs of its varied customers, but they *could* make it easy for customers and outside developers to do so. The value to SFDC is so considerable in terms of making its platform "sticky" to existing customers, as well as adding new ones, that it takes no royalty from apps it offers on the firm's AppExchange.

4. Pay Particular Attention to Customer-Created Apps

By "apps," I don't mean just software. I mean any modification to a product or service made by an outside entity, including customers themselves. For example, Ford developed the pickup truck after farmers began taking off the back end of their Model Ts and retrofitting them with wooden flatbed carriages in order to haul equipment. Ford began by introducing a one-ton conversion Model T chassis to accommodate the farmers, and when sales took off, Ford introduced the Model T Runabout in 1925. Henry Ford may not have asked customers what they wanted and was notorious for rejecting improvement ideas from his staff, but he was quite willing to accept the verdict of his customers and the marketplace.

More recently, insurance firm Aflac has designed a dozen apps for its seventy thousand sales employees to upload to their mobile phones. The apps help its salespeople access Aflac's customer database, policy information, claims information, and the like while on the road, freeing them from being tethered to the computer or a call center. Aflac is realizing substantial benefits in the form of improved sales productivity, as well as cost savings, as it reduces the calls made into the call center and frees up those employees to spend more time with customers or in processing insurance claims.

Similarly, mall operator General Growth Properties created an iPad app for its mall survey takers. The app allows them to enter customer responses directly into the iPad, which immediately uploads them to a computer, saving the time and expense of having data entry operators do so.

For a sales enablement or CRM firm serving the insurance, property management, or related markets, apps developed by customers (as opposed to noncustomer developers) have huge business potential, as we'll see shortly. That's why Apple, despite its closed innovation culture and initial reluctance to open up its platforms to app developers, now proactively sends its engineers out to college campuses to train students on how to develop apps. Clearly the firm has begun to recognize that powerful innovations can come from a savvy group of passionate and sophisticated customers.

Next we'll look at how to bring customers into your design process—and how one famously innovative firm does it.

Bringing Customers into Your Innovation Process

When biographer Walter Isaacson asked Steve Jobs why the iPod crushed Microsoft's competitor product, the Zune, Jobs told him:

> *The older I get, the more I see how much motivation matters. The Zune was crappy because people at Microsoft don't really love music or art the way we do.* We won because we personally love music. We made the iPod for ourselves, *and when you're doing something for yourself or your best friend or family, you're not going to cheese out. If you don't love something you're not going to go the extra mile, work the extra weekend, challenge the status quo as much.*[4] *{Emphasis added.}*

To be sure, in a famous picture taken of a young, newly wealthy Steve Jobs in his house, he's sitting on the floor of a large room with no furniture other than a lamp. He was so famously picky about design that he couldn't find furniture that was up to his standards. But there *is* a stereo, plopped on the floor—a sign of how passionate he was about music throughout his life, and of why Jobs himself was the iPod's best customer.

The trick for the rest of us, then, who aren't Steve Jobs, is to find those passionate customers and let them help design what they want to buy. Indeed, the ultimate goal is to redefine the innovation process to allow customers to play more of a role in areas where they have greater competence than your internal developers do.

The Hidden Innovators All Around You

Not every company can hire customers or potential customers of the products and services it provides. But companies can do much more to find and bring key customers into their innovation and product development processes to dramatically improve them, as an array of research by MIT's Eric von Hippel and others shows.

First, customers *want* to participate in developing improvements to the products and services they use. In a broad survey of people in the United Kingdom, 4.2 percent reported modifying a product in order to "make it better" for them, 1.4 percent reported *creating* a product, and 0.6 percent reported doing both. That translates into 2.9 million customers in the United Kingdom who are innovating to meet household needs. One said he attached a hook to a fishing pole to pull treetops to the ground in order to trim them. Another jerry-rigged a washing machine circuit to create a "spin only" cycle.

Second, customers themselves are often a better source than companies are of successful and even breakthrough innovation—and that's true in high-tech, mid-tech, and low-tech businesses. More specifically, "users" (individuals or firms who expect to benefit from *using* a product or service, as opposed to benefiting from selling it) develop many if not most of the commercially successful innovations in a range of industries. In some fields, they develop more than half of the products that eventually succeed.[5] For example, we've seen that farmers in effect developed the pickup truck for Ford. A Midwestern farmer also developed the modern self-propelled, center-pivot irrigation system that solved the problem of watering rolling terrain.

Moreover, von Hippel found that in the chemical industry, users developed 70 percent of the successful chemical processes and process equipment available for license. Forty-three percent of the major petroleum processing innovations were developed by users (and only 14 percent came from manufacturers—the rest came from other sources). Eighty-five percent of all pultrusion processing machinery innovations first introduced commercially from 1940 to 1976 came from users. The vast majority of scientific instrument innovations come from users, and between 1944 and 1962 between 25 percent and 33 percent of computer innovations were user designed.

Formal studies for consumer products haven't been done, but as von Hippel points out, consumers tinkering with concoctions for their own use have created products that went on to become highly successful commercially—such as Granola, Gatorade, sports bras, "grunge" clothing, mountain bikes, and skateboards. Bose engineers discovered quite by chance a group of top musicians performing at a club who were pointing the back of their Bose speakers toward the audience. When the engineers pointed that out, the musicians replied, "Yeah, we know, but it sounds much better." Being engineers, they ran some tests that confirmed the musicians' opinion, which led to a major new line of business: speakers for musicians to use in public concerts.[6]

The point is that users without commercial ambitions came up with many of these innovations—they stood to gain great benefits (at least at first) not from selling them but from *using* them for doing a better job of meeting their needs. Companies who take advantage of that kind of user behavior have much to gain. 3M provides an excellent case in point.

Lessons from 3M: Don't Leave Breakthrough Discoveries to Chance

The question that any business needs to ask is, "Are customers and other users developing significant innovations in our industry, or even at our own company? And if not, can we encourage them to do so?" It's worth making inquiries. Roger Lacey, vice president of 3M Company's Telecom Division, asked long-time employees how its early products were developed. They told him that some of its most successful products—such as "insulation displacement" systems for simultaneously splicing multiple telephone circuits—had come from prototype products developed by technicians working for telephone-operating companies. In other words, such products were being developed by the firm's customers.

Further, other technicians in these companies then adopted many of these innovations themselves. That is, in addition to designing and building the innovation, the lead users helped to prove the viability of their innovations in the marketplace.[7] For companies that can find and engage with such lead users, the potential payoff is tremendous. That got Lacey and others thinking: Why should 3M leave such discoveries to serendipity?

The opportunity to take a more intentional approach to lead-user innovation came when 3M's Medical-Surgical Markets Division went through a period of stagnating sales and declining margins in the 1990s. This occurred despite the robustness of the healthcare market, 3M's proven prowess at product innovation, and reams of market research data.

Based on the research being conducted by MIT's von Hippel and others, a 3M team proposed a last-gasp project: to bypass the internal innovation process and search for breakthrough innovations being created by outside users. The new product lines that resulted from the search were so successful that senior management authorized pursuit of additional lead-user projects over the next few years. When the results were compared with ordinary product development projects at 3M, the differences were dramatic: lead-user innovations resulted in new products that were significantly more novel than the others and achieved an average revenue of $146 million dollars in their fifth year, compared with $18 million for non-lead-user innovations. That led to a revolution in the way 3M does innovation. (See table 8-1.)

The growth of the Internet and social media is making it easier for firms that are looking to dramatically improve innovation to adopt the 3M process. Cisco Systems, a once highly innovative firm whose

TABLE 8-1

3M lead-user innovations

	Lead-user product concepts ($n = 5$)	Non-lead-user product concepts ($n = 42$)
Probability of success	80%	66%
Estimated sales in year 5	$146 million	$18 million
Percent market share in year 5	68%	33%
Novelty of product, compared to competition*	9.6	6.8

* Rated by 3M on a scale from 1 to 10.

Should Your Company Innovate by Working with Lead Users?

When considering whether it makes sense to find and work with lead users, you'll need to think through some of the issues involved. Conducting a lead-user project does require funding and time—3M's medical division required a team of four members working fifteen to twenty hours per week for four months to come up with new products suitable to propose to management. Of course, when the result is a series of innovations each worth an average of nine-figure sales, such a process can be a great investment. (See figure.)

Here are important factors to consider in making the call:

- Breakthrough lead-user innovations are more likely to succeed in rapidly growing markets. That's because businesses in such markets aren't able to keep up with the needs of lead users on the cutting edge of important trends, forcing these users to design add-ons or other adaptations themselves.

- Breakthrough lead-user innovations are more likely in heterogeneous markets, where customers have a wide variety of different needs and uses for your products or solutions, again making it unlikely for businesses serving them to keep up with them all.

attempts at growth by acquisition have stalled in the last few years, is looking for its next billion-dollar business from its iPrize competition, a process that closely follows 3M's lead-user process and adapts it to the Internet. Expect to see more of this. (See the sidebar "Should Your Company Innovate by Working with Lead Users?")

How to Find and Leverage Lead Users

Who are the people outside your firm who can best help you find breakthrough, high-value innovations?[8] First, lead users are not necessarily customers who are vocal participants in your communi-

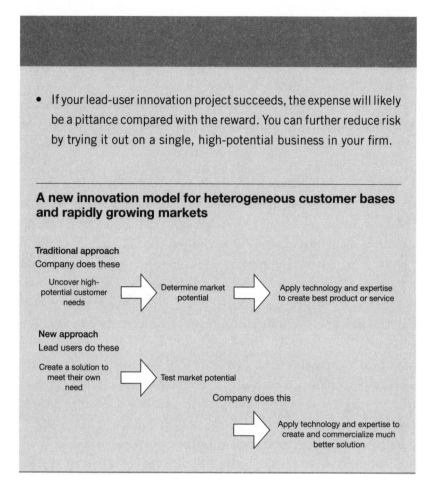

- If your lead-user innovation project succeeds, the expense will likely be a pittance compared with the reward. You can further reduce risk by trying it out on a single, high-potential business in your firm.

A new innovation model for heterogeneous customer bases and rapidly growing markets

Traditional approach
Company does these

Uncover high-potential customer needs

Determine market potential

Apply technology and expertise to create best product or service

New approach
Lead users do these

Create a solution to meet their own need

Test market potential

Company does this

Apply technology and expertise to create and commercialize much better solution

ties or frequent contributors on your blog or community Web sites. They may not even be *your* customers at all (although your customers can help you find them). In some cases, they may even be from another industry, as we'll see.

A lead user is someone who is ahead of the market with respect to an important market trend and would gain substantial benefits from a solution to the needs he has encountered there. In many cases, the benefits to be gained are so high that the lead user will go to the trouble of adapting existing products in order to develop his own solution. Because lead users are at the forefront of market trends, it's a reasonable bet that the solutions they develop will have broad appeal and generate high returns for the company that converts them into something it can sell. Research by von Hippel and others bears this out.

The question then is: How do you find these special people, tap into their knowledge, and turn that knowledge into a product or service?

1. FORM THE RIGHT TEAM Effective lead-user teams should be cross-disciplinary, including both marketing and technical people. The 3M medical project team, for example, consisted of four people, including a chemist with a PhD (who was team leader), a technical expert, a manufacturing expert, and a marketing expert. All had reputations for innovative, out-of-the-box thinking. In addition, the marketing expert was a former nurse with rich experience with hospital practices—in other words, she came from the world of the customer. They also had strong and active support from two senior management sponsors. And they established ties with key company stakeholder groups, realizing that their involvement and support from the start was key to having their ultimate recommendations taken seriously. Working with the stakeholders, the team began putting together preliminary ideas about the kinds of target markets they wanted to pursue, as well as the types of innovations they wanted to develop.

2. GET CLEAR ON INDUSTRY TRENDS By definition, lead users are working at the forefront of an important industry trend. Therefore, it's important to identify early on what industry trends are out there and which of those make sense for your company to investigate.

Some teams start this search for trends with industry publications to get a baseline of conventional wisdom on where the industry is headed—but that's probably a mistake. It can influence you to think like everyone else, which is not the best way to develop breakthrough ideas. 3M has developed a concept of *lead-use experts* in the marketplace. Note that these aren't necessarily vocal or prominent bloggers or other so-called opinion leaders. Instead, you're looking for genuine authorities on market and technical trends, as well as leading users of applications that have arisen to meet needs created by those trends.

Of course, finding such lead-use experts—like finding lead users themselves—isn't necessarily easy, since they're not necessarily the most visible or vocal people. The process *is* straightforward, however, using simple networking and the principle that people who have achieved a level of expertise in a field typically know who the people are who have *more* expertise, which allows you to "pyramid" to find the top people on the leading edge.

For example, among expert candidates initially contacted by the 3M medical products lead-user team were authors who had published major articles on infection in surgeries. The team also talked to researchers in academic settings, as well as prominent doctors and nurses at leading hospitals. Starting with these people, the team was then able to locate experts who met their criteria of "the best" in their fields. The 3M team then conducted thirty- to forty-five-minute interviews, mostly by telephone. The result was a clear understanding of the major trends in the industry.

From that understanding they identified the specific customer needs that would result from those trends. The team will refine and perhaps even change these needs as they talk directly with lead users, but it's critical that the team has that needs framework up front to keep the project focused.

When searching for lead users, don't forget to investigate users' analogue markets as well. Analogues are other markets whose customers have more extreme needs than yours do—and they are fertile ground for highly lucrative innovations. Automobile firms, for example, looking to make significant improvements to car braking systems, got the idea for antilock brakes from the aerospace industry. Secure braking systems in all kinds of conditions are important for cars, but they are absolutely essential for an airplane.

3. NEXT, FIND LEAD USERS You've found the experts. Now how do you find the customers and other users out there who are actually at the forefront of the trends you've identified, who have relevant

new product or service ideas, and who may have even developed prototypes?

For example, a hearing aid manufacturer that focused on severe hearing impairment wanted to develop a product for people with only mild hearing loss. In its research, the project team found that one emerging major trend was demand for higher-quality sound processing. So the team looked for lead users who could give them a clearer understanding of what attributes of "higher-quality" hearing were important to them.

The lead users they identified and engaged with included serious athletes competing in team sports who needed good hearing enhancement because of noisy crowds. They also talked to executives who needed to hear well in many different settings, such as restaurants, group meetings, and over the phone. A particularly valuable lead-user group was expert audiologists who were hearing aid users themselves; they were able to understand the limitations in existing products like no one else could. With that kind of information, the team was then able to generate preliminary concepts for new products and services.

Likewise, when generating your own preliminary design concepts, be sure you can answer some key questions, such as the following: What specific features and attributes will the new product or service have? What value will it provide customers? What forms of the new design does it make sense for our firm to create?

4. COLLABORATE WITH LEAD USERS Collaborating directly with lead users can clearly cure many of the ills that plague the usual innovation process. You're not *asking* customers to describe their needs or to state their preferences regarding possible new solutions that you propose. They've *already* identified a need so compelling that, in many cases, they've gone to the trouble of producing a solution and are using it—and in some cases, it is being used by others in the lead user's network. The need has been identified, solutions tried, and prototypes developed and perhaps even market tested.

Having identified lead users and lead-use experts, project teams can then bring them in for a workshop as a final step toward developing proposed new products or solutions that do an even better job for the user/customer. 3M's medical team, for example, had an ongoing list of concept development ideas that they refined throughout the first three stages of the project. For the in-person workshop, they selected lead users and lead-use experts who had the knowledge, skills, and experience that could fill in missing pieces and push concept development to a conclusion. Of course, project teams may need to remain open to development of exciting new concepts that may arise during dynamic exchanges of ideas in a live setting. By bringing together lead users with the firm project team, discussions of proposed new products can remain grounded in what's technically feasible and fits in with management's overarching objectives for the firm.

What I have just described is a rather straightforward process of innovation at 3M. But what it has meant for the company has been revolutionary: bringing lead users into its design process has resulted in new products that generated *eight times* the revenue of products developed through ordinary product development approaches.

As we've seen in this chapter, finding and engaging with customer innovators can be quite lucrative—as well as supremely satisfying and beneficial to customers themselves. If you can attract such customers and give them a way to help you innovate, you'll soon be attracting the all-important lead users of your designs.

In the next section I offer a conclusion to this book by describing how you can apply what you've read in these chapters directly to your own company's situation.

How to Use This Book to Accelerate Your Company's Growth

Now that you've read the book, you can begin applying its principles in two ways: for short-term growth goals and long-term goals.

In my experience, the best way to create a foundation of long-term organizational change needed to instill a culture based on customer engagement and advocacy is through a series of smaller successes that can be achieved quickly and with impressive results.

Here's a road map to get the process going:

1. Start with a product or solution, along with the market or markets, that presents the highest potential for growth for your firm. Consider who your most strategic customers are in these markets. A B2B firm may have just a relatively few prospective customers that can provide 50 percent or more of your projected growth, if you can start landing their business. On the other hand, if your highest growth potential is with small and medium business (SMB) customers, you're looking to penetrate a larger or even mass market.

2. Verify this. Make sure that those customers, whether larger enterprise firms or SMB firms, are indeed providing the sort of profitable growth you think they are. This is a critical sanity check and is relatively easy to perform with today's CRM systems. Often, firms find that among their customers in any particular market and line of business, only 20 percent or so are providing the lion's share of profits. For example, that enterprise customer you think is so valuable to your business may in fact be unprofitable due to demands that you provide steep price discounts and maintain high inventory levels at your expense.

Now that you've identified and verified who your most valuable customers are, and thus know whom to target, it's time for step 3.

3. Determine why you're falling short of reasonably achievable growth goals, and what needs to be done to correct the situation. Necessary corrective action might include one or two of the following:

- Doing a better job of getting the word out in your market about your products and services

- Penetrating high-potential new markets

- Improving or shoring up customer retention

- Improving success rates of new product and solution development or of product refreshes

- Creating more breakthrough innovations

- Selling more strategic solutions to higher levels of your customer organizations, perhaps even the C suite

- Improving sales-lead generation or close rates, or both

To help you with this, take the diagnostic test in the appendix of this text.

4. Now, with the help of this book, determine how your customers can assist you in taking the necessary corrective action. For example, suppose, upon taking the diagnostic, that you realize that you need to shore up declining retention rates (question 4) as a result of customers not understanding that your updated product can do a great job of meeting their new needs. Suppose you also need to do a better job of getting the word out to the larger market about what you do (question 6).

The diagnostic refers you to chapters 4, 5, and 6 of this book, where you'll be reminded, for example, how SAS Canada restored its traditionally high retention rates, after they had suffered a precipitous drop, by creating champion and super champion customers who did a superb job—much better than internal marketing and salespeople could have done—of communicating how SAS software could indeed meet needs that defecting customers didn't realize they could.

You'll also review how Hitachi Data Systems engaged very creatively with customers—in some ways much like SFDC does—to successfully get the word out about its offerings, overcome negative information disseminated by its much bigger, better-funded competition, and reverse a history of subpar performance from its new product releases.

As you review these cases, keep in mind two things:

- Let them stimulate your team's creativity, developing your own approaches to customer engagement and advocacy appropriate to your customers and market. And be ready to learn and refine as you go.

- Most important—if you do one thing recommended here, make this the one—every customer engagement and advocacy initiative you create must be formulated in terms of *an exceptional mutual value proposition with your customers.* It must provide great value to them and result in significant contributions to your growth and profitability. That's how to make them sustainable. For example, the SAS Canada champion and super champion customer advocates expanded their peer networks and gained recognition that enhanced their careers and standing in their professional community, helped them develop leadership and speaking skills, and the like.

5. As your teams organize and implement customer engagement initiatives, an effective senior executive should remain involved and supportive of the efforts. This doesn't mean making the occasional appearance at meetings or conferences. It does mean an executive who's capable of making sure (and has the clout to do so) that the various customer initiatives you launch meet the following criteria:

- Are well integrated with each other and with other relevant areas of marketing, sales, and product development

- Exploit the synergies that will develop among these initiatives—and there will be a lot of these

- Receive necessary support and cooperation from these other relevant departments

- Present a holistic picture to the customer, in the customer's terms and aligned with her thinking

- Provide exceptional value to customers, and a significant return to the business

---

Today's economy demands a better way to secure robust organic growth than companies have relied on in the past. In this book I have described that better way—one that goes beyond the limited purview of customer-as-buyer to show you how to unlock the value of customer relationships in all of the firm's growth processes: from product development to marketing and sales and other internal resources.

The new customer value proposition I have described engages, organizes, and leverages the force of your own customer base to propel sustained growth—all while creating far greater value for customers themselves. That is how companies that adapt most successfully to an increasingly connected world will begin to reimagine their source of true wealth creation.

Key Tasks

How to Get Meaningful Customer Input to Make Dramatic Improvements in New Product Development.

- Customers are a superb, and often overlooked, source of product development and innovation. Remember: you have more customers than you have internal product developers; customers understand other customers like them better than you do; and they have more credibility with other customers as well. Learn to leverage those facts.

- Look for and engage with customers who have something that other customers want—resources, knowledge, data, expertise plus a willingness to help each other, and the like.

- Look for ways to turn your company into a customer design platform—so that customers can create their own experience, with your help.

- Pay particular attention to customer-created apps (and that can mean more than just software).

- Consider integrating lead-user innovation into your firm—it can be less expensive yet far more lucrative than traditional innovation processes.

Are You Creating Robust Organic Growth?

A Diagnostic

THE EXECUTIVE SUITE sometimes overlooks organic growth, focusing instead on the next attractive acquisition. Yet acquisitions seldom pay off financially for the acquiring firm, and even when they do, at some point the firm has to achieve organic growth for the organization it winds up with.

What follows is a diagnostic to help you determine how effectively you're engaging customer advocates in the growth process.

Scoring: If you find that your average score in any particular category is less than five or six, it may indicate an opportunity to engage with customers to dramatically improve organic growth for your firm.

1. Organic Growth: The Starting Point

(See chapter 2)

Do you know who your most profitable customers are (based on financial data that includes revenue generated by individual customer purchases as well as costs, including cost of capital, allocated by individual customer or at least by customer segment)? Note that if you haven't actually run the numbers, your assumption about who your most profitable customers are may well be wrong.

Not at all					To some extent					Yes
0	1	2	3	4	5	6	7	8	9	10

Regarding your referring customers, do you know (again, based on financial data) which customers provide the most valuable referrals? Note that many companies assume their most profitable purchasing customers are *also* their best source of referrals. That's typically *not* true.

Not at all					To some extent					Yes
0	1	2	3	4	5	6	7	8	9	10

2. Building Marquee Customer Accounts

(See chapter 7)

As a baseline, do you know how profitable your marquee customers actually are?[1]

Not at all					To some extent					Yes
0	1	2	3	4	5	6	7	8	9	10

How many of your marquee customers do you systematically engage with regularly—in the form of customer advisory boards (CABs) or executive forums or both—to keep abreast of their challenges and needs, as well as to gain feedback and input on your offerings and your firm's direction and strategy?

None at all					To some extent					Regularly
0	1	2	3	4	5	6	7	8	9	10

What significant ideas have you implemented from your CAB or forum in the last six months?

None at all			**We're planning one or two**				**We've implemented two or more**			
0	1	2	3	4	5	6	7	8	9	10

What share of wallet have you captured from your CAB or executive forum customers, compared with other customers?

No difference				**Somewhat more**				**Significantly more**		
0	1	2	3	4	5	6	7	8	9	10

How does your profitable growth of these accounts compare with over-all profitable growth?

No difference				**Somewhat more**				**Significantly more**		
0	1	2	3	4	5	6	7	8	9	10

3. Getting the Sale

(See chapter 3)

How often do salespeople have the customer references or testimonials they need to attract prospects and close deals?

Rarely				**Sometimes**					**Always**	
0	1	2	3	4	5	6	7	8	9	10

Can your sales and marketing people find relevant customer references when they need them?

Rarely				**Sometimes**					**Always**	
0	1	2	3	4	5	6	7	8	9	10

How long, on average, does it take them to find such references if they're "in your system"?

More than a day					Hours					Minutes
0	1	2	3	4	5	6	7	8	9	10

How many of your once-enthusiastic customer references have you lost due to burnout or other frustration with your customer reference process?

Too many					Some (enough to hurt)					None
0	1	2	3	4	5	6	7	8	9	10

4. Customer Retention

(See chapter 4)

No matter how many new customers you bring in the front door, it's tough to grow if the old ones are leaving through the back door.

What are the retention rates for your key business lines? What are you doing to increase customer retention rates?

Unacceptable					Acceptable for our industry					Highest in our industry
0	1	2	3	4	5	6	7	8	9	10

Do you and your employees understand how your offerings contribute to the success of your customers?

Poorly					To some extent					Extremely well
0	1	2	3	4	5	6	7	8	9	10

Do you perform regular "sanity checks" to make sure that, when asked, customers would give the same answer?

Never					Sometimes					Regularly
0	1	2	3	4	5	6	7	8	9	10

How much are you engaging customers in the effort, for example, to help other customers understand and use new offerings you provide that they may not be aware of?

Not at all					To some extent				Regularly and effectively	
0	1	2	3	4	5	6	7	8	9	10

5. Innovation and New Product Development

(See chapter 8)

How well are you uncovering and meeting new customer needs? What's the success rate of your new product and service development efforts?

Unacceptable				Acceptable for our industry				Highest in our industry		
0	1	2	3	4	5	6	7	8	9	10

How well are you engaging with customers in such efforts? Are you able, like Salesforce.com, to engage with poorly serviced customers in a market and develop a successful, perhaps disruptive, innovation to serve them better?

Not at all					To some extent					Yes
0	1	2	3	4	5	6	7	8	9	10

Are you able, like 3M, to find and engage with cutting-edge lead users to dramatically improve the ROI of your innovation efforts?

Not at all					To some extent					Yes
0	1	2	3	4	5	6	7	8	9	10

6. Branding and Getting the Word Out

(See chapters 4, 5, and 6)

Customers are your most credible spokespeople.

In your efforts to develop new offerings for the market, and to get the word out about them—particularly those that your market wouldn't necessarily expect from you—can you accurately determine how many customer references you'll need to help build media awareness and close deals in order to meet sales forecasts?

Not at all					To some extent					Yes
0	1	2	3	4	5	6	7	8	9	10

In your product development efforts, are you able to find beta customers who are already passionate about your existing offerings and are highly likely to provide referrals, references, and positive word of mouth for the new one?

Not at all					To some extent					Yes
0	1	2	3	4	5	6	7	8	9	10

In your efforts to penetrate new markets, are you engaging effectively online with influencers in those markets?

Poorly				**Acceptable in our market**				**Best in our market**		
0	1	2	3	4	5	6	7	8	9	10

To what extent are they creating awareness for your firm and its offerings?

Poorly				**Acceptable in our market**				**Best in our market**		
0	1	2	3	4	5	6	7	8	9	10

To what extent are they creating leads?

Poorly				**Acceptable in our market**				**Best in our market**		
0	1	2	3	4	5	6	7	8	9	10

In your efforts to brand and get the word out about your offerings, how well is your core of passionate customers supporting these efforts?

Poorly				**Acceptable in our market**				**Best in our market**		
0	1	2	3	4	5	6	7	8	9	10

7. Mastering Community Marketing

(See chapter 6)

If you have a substantial core of passionate customers who are enthusiastic about the prospect of talking to others about your firm and its products and services, how well do you measure and influence the business impact of their doing so?

Not at all				**To some extent**				**With precision**		
0	1	2	3	4	5	6	7	8	9	10

To what extent are such efforts contributing to lead generation, brand awareness, or sales-close rates, as companies such as Intel and Salesforce.com are doing?

Not at all					To some extent				Best in our industry	
0	1	2	3	4	5	6	7	8	9	10

For Your Live Events

Do you create live events to provide customers a range of opportunities to interact with each other and with prospects?

Not at all					To some extent					Yes
0	1	2	3	4	5	6	7	8	9	10

Do you know how many prospects attend such events and how many of those become customers? Do you know what the close rates are and the cost of closing, versus other sales approaches?

Not at all					To some extent				Yes, with precision	
0	1	2	3	4	5	6	7	8	9	10

Can you identify three things you've learned in the last year that have improved your outcomes for such events, in terms of lowering costs, making them easier to execute, attracting prospects to attend, and increasing close rates?

Not at all					Maybe one or two					Yes
0	1	2	3	4	5	6	7	8	9	10

In your efforts to develop thought leadership in your market, how effectively are your internal thought leaders engaging with your customer communities?

Not at all					To some extent				Best in our industry	
0	1	2	3	4	5	6	7	8	9	10

How well do you measure engagement: comments, downloads, click-throughs, leads created, sales?

Not at all					To some extent				Best in class	
0	1	2	3	4	5	6	7	8	9	10

8. Gaining Mastery of the Web and Social Media

(See chapters 5 and 6)

Attract notice and build leads through your Web site.

How much of your Web site material is about your customers and how your offerings are making them successful as opposed to about you, written by your employees or agencies?

Less than 10%									More than 70%	
0	1	2	3	4	5	6	7	8	9	10

Do you test for and determine the optimal mix of customer content on your site—such as testimonials, case studies, articles, aggregated customer outcomes, or results data?

Not at all				To some extent				Yes, regularly and with precision		
0	1	2	3	4	5	6	7	8	9	10

Do you test for the optimal mix of formats in terms of generating customer and prospect engagement—such as video, Webinars, text, graphics, interactive games?

Not at all				To some extent				Yes, regularly and with precision		
0	1	2	3	4	5	6	7	8	9	10

In Your Social Media Efforts

Do you know who the influencers (a category of customer) are in your market, are you successfully engaging with them, and do you know how much revenue they are driving?

Not at all				To some extent				Yes, with precision		
0	1	2	3	4	5	6	7	8	9	10

Do you measure the engagement created by your own thought leadership efforts on the Web—whether created by your own internal experts or customer content?[2]

Not at all				To some extent				Yes, with precision		
0	1	2	3	4	5	6	7	8	9	10

Do you know how much revenue and profits or other value are created by your online communities?

Not at all				To some extent				Yes, with precision		
0	1	2	3	4	5	6	7	8	9	10

What contributions have these communities made to new product development or apps development?

Not at all		To some extent						Significant—and growing—contributions		
0	1	2	3	4	5	6	7	8	9	10

9. Creating a Better Customer Value Proposition

(See chapters 1, 2, and 7)

How much have you expanded the value proposition you provide to your customers—*beyond* the value of your products and services?

Not at all				To some extent				Best in our industry		
0	1	2	3	4	5	6	7	8	9	10

How much have you expanded the value you harvest *from* customers—*beyond* the money they pay for your products and services? (For example, with measures such as customer referral value or customer influencer value.)

Not at all				To some extent				Best in our industry		
0	1	2	3	4	5	6	7	8	9	10

NOTES

Chapter 1

1. See, for example, Frederick F. Reichheld, *The Ultimate Question: Driving Good Profits and True Growth* (Boston: Harvard Business School Press, 2006), *The Ultimate Question 2.0: How Net-Promoter Companies Thrive in a Customer-Driven World* (Boston: Harvard Business Review Press, 2011), and *The Loyalty Effect: The Hidden Force Behind Growth, Profits, and Lasting Value* (Boston: Harvard Business School Press, 2001); Joseph Pine II and James H. Gilmore, *The Experience Economy: Work Is Theatre and Every Business a Stage* (Boston: Harvard Business School Press, 1999); and Don Peppers and Martha Rogers, *The One to One Manager: Real-World Lessons in Customer Relationship Management* (New York: Currency/Doubleday, 1999), and *Enterprise One to One: Tools for Competing in the Interactive Age* (New York: Currency/Doubleday, 1997).

2. In the Net Promoter Score (NPS) methodology, a "promoter" is someone who says on a survey that he or she would be highly likely to recommend a firm to a colleague or friend.

3. The information on Salesforce.com here and in subsequent chapters is based on Marc Benioff's excellent book *Behind the Cloud: The Untold Story of How Salesforce.com Went from Idea to Billion-Dollar Company—and Revolutionized an Industry* (San Francisco: Jossey-Bass, 2009) and on conversations with several executives and managers at Salesforce.com, some of whom have participated in our conferences.

4. Sean Geehan, presentation to the 2009 Summit on Customer Engagement, based on research performed by the Geehan Group. See chapter 7.

Chapter 2

1. Firms that implement NPS often do little, if anything, to actually encourage their promoters to go forth and promote. As it turns out, just because customers *say* they'd be likely to refer you doesn't mean they actually *do* so. Customers of a telecommunications and of a financial services firm, for example, expressed their intention to provide referrals in large numbers: 81 percent for the telecom and 68 percent for the financial services firm. Yet when you look at how many actually did so and how many of the referrals actually became customers—and, of those, how many became *profitable* customers—the numbers dwindle to about 10 percent of customers in both firms. V. Kumar, Andrew Petersen, and Robert P. Leone, "How Valuable Is Word of Mouth?" *Harvard Business Review,* October 2007, 139–146.

Chapter 3

1. See chapter 6 for more on customer communities.

2. Joshua Horwitz and Katy Boos, *The Customer Reference Handbook* (San Jose, CA/Boulder, CO: BigSky Communications/Boulder Logic, 2009); http://customerreferencehandbook.com.

Chapter 4

1. Alan Weiss, author of dozens of books on consulting and other business topics and consultant to major corporations such as Hewlett-Packard, Merck, Toyota, the *New York Times,* and many others, is today arguably the world's top thought leader on consulting. His global community of consultants—of which I'm a member—meets regularly at live summits and workshops, and online in Weiss's forums. The concepts of marketing gravity and the accelerant curve were developed by Weiss and his community and are constantly being updated and refined. See also Alan Weiss, *The Consulting Bible: Everything You Need to Know to Create and Expand a Seven-Figure Consulting Practice* (Hoboken, NJ: Wiley, 2011).

2. Also developed by Alan Weiss and his community. See previous note.

3. Microsoft won't disclose how many MVPs are customers and how many aren't, for obvious reasons. Key to an MVP's influence in the market is maintaining a position of neutrality. "We accept—and realize it's necessary, in fact—that our MVPs will sometimes say unfavorable things about us," Portillo says.

Chapter 5

1. Author conversation with a vice president of marketing for the division.

2. "The Rise of the Digital C-Suite: How Executives Locate and Filter Business Information," Forbes Insights in association with Google, 2009.

3. The "I'm in Dell Hell" story is well told in Charlene Li and Josh Bernoff, *Groundswell: Winning in a World Transformed by Social Technologies* (Boston: Harvard Business Press, 2008), 205–211. Many of these firms turn such manageable issues—which are often opportunities to deepen relationships—into disasters by applying old-school marketing and communications approaches.

4. See, for example, "SiriusDecisions," B2B Buyer's Survey, 2010.

5. We'll look more closely at community building and social media in chapter 6.

6. Those ratios have become standard for many firms.

7. Badly chastened, Dell has now become a model for its ability to communicate and respond to customers on the Web.

8. See http://blog.customerreferenceforum.com/crf/2010/10/customer-reference-video-watch.html.

9. David Weinberger, *Everything Is Miscellaneous: The Power of the New Digital Disorder* (New York: Times Books, 2007).

10. For example, the scientific journal *Nature* showed that entries in the online, community-generated encyclopedia *Wikipedia* are just as likely to be accu-

rate as corresponding entries in the traditionally hierarchical *Encyclopaedia Britannica*. See Jim Giles, "Internet Encyclopaedias Go Head to Head," *Nature* 438, no. 900–901 (2005).

11. Blog post by Christophe Bertrand, HDS, February 25, 2010, http://blogs.hds.com/christophe/2010/02/validating-the-technology.html.

Chapter 6

1. Thomas J. Peters and Robert H. Waterman Jr., *In Search of Excellence: Lessons from America's Best-Run Companies* (New York: Harper & Row, 1982).

2. William G. Lee, *Mavericks in the Workplace: Harnessing the Genius of American Workers* (New York: Oxford University Press, 1998).

3. Alexis de Tocqueville, *Democracy in America* (London: Saunders and Otley, 1832). Still regarded as perhaps the most perceptive account of how and why the American experiment succeeded.

4. Immigrants took to community building as rapidly as the Americans who preceded them, with organizations such as the Sons of Poland, Sons of Norway, and Sons of Italy proliferating.

5. Robert Putnam, *Bowling Alone: The Collapse and Revival of American Community* (New York: Simon & Schuster, 2000), 171–172.

6. Lee, *Mavericks in the Workplace.*

7. Ronald S. Burt, *Brokerage and Closure: An Introduction to Social Capital* (New York: Oxford University Press, 2005).

8. David T. Beito, *From Mutual Aid to the Welfare State: Fraternal Societies and Social Services, 1890–1967* (Chapel Hill, NC: University of North Carolina Press, 2000).

9. Wong is now CEO of Eventley, a SFDC spinoff that makes a community-building platform available to other firms—a recognition of the exceptional value it provides.

10. I include the act of finding because as we've seen, it's a mistake to think that you already know who these people are. Even customers you think are references may not be references at all, as we saw with SAP in chapter 3.

Chapter 7

1. See Andrew Sobel, *All for One: 10 Strategies for Building Trusted Client Partnerships* (Hoboken, NJ: Wiley, 2009). Sobel, a colleague of mine, is the world's preeminent expert on building long-term relationships with senior executives.

2. 2010 IBM global survey of 1,500 CEOs.

3. The most recent research on this appears to be G. A. Stevens and J. Burley, "3,000 Raw Ideas = 1 Commercial Success!" *Research Technology Management* 40, no. 3 (May–June 1997).

4. See chapter 1.

Chapter 8

1. Greg A. Stevens and James Burley, "Piloting the Rocket of Radical Innovation," *Research Technology Management* 46 (March–April 2003): 16–25. Of course, what matters for any company is the rate of *its* innovation successes.

2. As Henry Ford supposedly said (and Steve Jobs liked to repeat), "If I had asked customers what they wanted, they'd have said a faster horse."

3. 2010 IBM global CEO study (based on input from 1,500 CEOs).

4. Walter Isaacson, *Steve Jobs* (New York: Simon & Schuster, 2011), 407.

5. Eric von Hippel, *Democratizing Innovation* (Cambridge, MA: MIT Press, 2005), 19–22.

6. Joan Churchill, Eric von Hippel, and Mary Sonnack, *Lead User Project Handbook: A Practical Guide for Lead User Project Teams,* 2009; http://web.mit .edu/evhippel/www/Lead%20User%20Project%20Handbook%20%28Full%20 Version%29.pdf.

7. A *lead user* is someone on the leading edge of a trend in the marketplace who makes changes to a product that he or she hopes to benefit from using personally.

8. This section is based on conversations with Eric von Hippel and former executives at 3M, as well as on Churchill, von Hippel, and Sonnack, *Lead User Project Handbook.*

Appendix

1. A working, conceptual definition of marquee customer accounts for B2B firms can be those relatively few customers who generate the lion's share of your profitable revenues. Some firms include those larger accounts in new, strategically important markets.

2. "Engagement" means that the visitor took some action: clicked a link, downloaded a white paper, contacted your firm, or so forth.

INDEX

Note: Page numbers followed by *f* refer to figures; page numbers followed by *t* refer to tables.

ACKNOWLEDGMENTS

I've been blessed with the support of a terrific network, and many of these people have contributed essential information and insights for this book.

Thanks to my colleague Amanda Setili for her invaluable insights—she got the concept immediately, the title was her idea, and her input in chapter 2 was (that word again) essential.

Thanks to Patty Morrison—a dream customer for many of the firms mentioned in this book—for so freely sharing with me and my community of customer advocacy professionals what it takes to attract a dream customer and then get that customer to advocate for you.

Thanks to über-consultant and thought leader Alan Weiss. When I told Alan I had an idea for a book and asked him to please shoot it down (which he's quite good at doing), he surprised me by saying it was a superb idea and proceeded to help me put together an outline on the spot.

Thanks to my entire Customer Reference Forum community, which inspired many of the case studies that wound up in the book. Its members attend our conferences, share what their customer advocacy programs are doing (which is often amazing), serve on our Advisory Board, mentor each other, and much more. Special thanks to Abby Atkinson, Rhett Livengood, Wally Thiessen, and Michael Stephenson for ideas and experiences that made it into the book.

Thanks also to other colleagues and clients who contributed great ideas and experiences: Jackie Breiter, Dawn Cochran, Connie Dean, Sugato Deb, Steve Ellis, Chris Fleck, Coleen Kaiser, John Pasquarette, Leif Pederson, Nestor Portillo, Rich Stanfield, and Tom Wong. Special thanks to:

- Brian Householder and Asim Zaheer at Hitachi Data Systems. Asim has provided some great insights into the role customer advocacy is playing at HDS that enriched one of our Summits as well as this book. My lunches with Brian opened a window into how one of the world's most talented senior marketing executives thinks about customer advocates (and it starts with customer value).

- Brad O'Neil, a visionary entrepreneur who is pioneering highly successful approaches to capturing customer advocacy content, as his firm's rapidly growing list of marquee clients will attest.

- My good friend and small groups compadre, Julia Welborn— one of the most talented executives I've had the pleasure to know, and more important, a great person and mom.

- My editor at Harvard Business Review Press, Jeff Kehoe, a fine editor and good guy who's been a joy to work with, along with the outstanding staff at *Harvard Business Review.*

- And to my fabulous agents, Ike Williams and Katherine Flynn.

ABOUT THE AUTHOR

BILL LEE helps organizations reinvent customer relationships and accelerate growth through the creation of engaged, passionate customer communities. He pioneered the concept that return on relationship is the key to organic growth in organizations of any size, public or private.

His firm, Lee Consulting Group, has assembled some of the world's top experts, who bring experience from leading consulting firms such as McKinsey, Bain, and Booz Allen Hamilton, along with industry and public sector experience from organizations such as Kimberly-Clark, eBay, Mitsubishi, and the Department of Defense. The firm specializes in strategy, organizational performance improvement, execution, customer community building, market analysis, international growth, and business model innovation.

For the last eight years, Bill has built vibrant communities of customer engagement professionals. His industry-leading conferences include the Summit on Customer Engagement, Customer Reference Forum, Summit on Customer Communities, and CAB Exchange Summit. These conferences have attracted many of the world's leading global firms, such as Microsoft, Apple, Oracle, Dell, EMC, SAP, Red Hat, Wells Fargo, Salesforce.com, SAS Institute, AmerisourceBergen Corporation, Research In Motion, AT&T, Alcatel-Lucent, IBM, Siemens, and many others.

A former teaching fellow at Stanford University, Bill was a law clerk for a federal judge in Washington, DC. He also worked with a team that formulated presidential campaign positions on sensitive legal and policy issues. As an official in the Department of Defense (Office of the Secretary), Bill gained insight into what it takes to effect change in the largest, most complex organization in the world. He served as vice president of operations for a prominent Dallas-based commercial construction firm and controller at a major recreational boat manufacturer.

Bill is the author of *Mavericks in the Workplace: Harnessing the Genius of American Workers* and has written for a number of publications, including the *Wall Street Journal*, *Management Review*, *Organizational Dynamics*, *Executive Excellence*, and others.